COMMERCIAL REAL ESTATE: JOURNEY TOWARDS FINANCIAL FREEDOM

What Everyone Ought To Know About Commercial Real Estate in 3 Simple Steps

MICHAEL STEVEN

michael@TheBestSellerBooks.com

© **Copyright 2020 - All rights reserved.**

The content contained within this book may not be reproduced, duplicated, or transmitted without direct written permission from the author or the publisher.

For more information:

Website: VAGPublishing.com

Email: michael@TheBestSellerBooks.com

Under no circumstances will any blame or legal responsibility be held against the publisher, or author, for any damages, reparation, or monetary loss due to the information contained within this book. Either directly or indirectly. You are responsible for your own choices, actions, and results.

Legal Notice:

This book is copyright protected. This book is only for personal use. You cannot amend, distribute, sell, use, quote or paraphrase any part, or the content within this book, without the consent of the author or publisher.

Disclaimer Notice:

Please note the information contained within this document is for educational purposes only. All effort has been executed to present accurate, up to date, and reliable, complete information. No warranties of any kind are declared or implied. Readers acknowledge that the author is not engaging in the rendering of legal, financial, medical, or professional advice. The content within this book has been derived from various sources. Please consult a licensed professional before attempting any techniques outlined in this book.

By reading this document, the reader agrees that under no circumstances is the author responsible for any losses, direct or indirect, which are incurred as a result of the use of the information contained within this document, including, but not limited to, — errors, omissions, or inaccuracies.

CONTENTS

Real Estate Investment Checklist	v
Introduction	vii
Chapter One: Commercial Real Estate - How Can I Benefit From What it Has to Offer?	1
Chapter Two: Planning Your Strategy for Commercial Real Estate Investing	19
Chapter Three: Step One, Part One - Study the Market	43
Chapter Four: Step One, Part Two - Study the Property	66
Chapter Five: Step Two - The Means, The Support, and The Structure of Your Investment	78
Chapter Six: Step Three - Managing and Maintaining Your Investments	98
Conclusions and Glossary	112
Final Words	117
Check Out My Other Books!	119
Real Estate Investment Checklist	121
References	123

REAL ESTATE INVESTMENT CHECKLIST

(9 Calculators That Will Help You Achieve Success!)

This checklist includes:

❏ 9 important calculators that you should use to achieve success and head towards *Financial Freedom with Real Estate*

❏ Helpful links

❏ Plus receive future updates

Forget about yesterday and start thinking about tomorrow.

"The past and the future are separated by a second, so make that second count!" ~ *Quote from Carmine Pirone*

To receive your Free Real Estate Calculators Checklist, email me at:

michael@TheBestSellerBooks.com

INTRODUCTION

✣✣✣

'Investments' seem to be the new buzz word in conversations of late. You hear it in the workplace, you see it on your social feed, and your friend is boasting of the windfall they just cashed in on. With the economy in such a precarious form of late, most people are searching for financial stability with greater security and independence. This would allow one to be able to weather any downward spiral or unexpected but inevitable economic changes in the future.

In other words, we want financial freedom.

Commercial real estate (CRE) has been a favorite of savvy investors for many years, often attracting only the rich and well-connected due to the high initial buy-ins of CRE. Even 20 years ago, few people had the sizable investment wallet needed to fund any land or property investment worth $250,000 or more.

As we move into the third decade of the 21st century, however, things have changed. Not only can a modest investment be made in a CRE scheme, but that same small investment can make double-digit profits from many of these modest initiatives. The unfair advantage of needing great wealth has been removed, and even low to middle-income families can put $500 into a crowd-funding group to generate passive income for their retirement years.

But it can be more lucrative than this.

You don't have to wait 20 years to make great money in CRE. With the ability to finance loans, renovate run-down buildings, join like-minded investment groups, or own and then rent as you improve your wealth strategies, anyone can begin in CRE investing. Creative options and financial institutions' collateral-based lending, aligned with a few well-thought-out strategies, can bring passive income your way within months!

This wealth isn't just stated on your financial quarterly report - it's actually cash-in-your-pocket wealth, the kind that can propel you to financial freedom!

You may already have a good idea of how you want to invest your hard-earned dollars and are looking to diversify your financial profile and portfolio with real estate. Perhaps you are looking to begin small, testing the waters of CRE to see if you can make a decent return on your money before committing your entire savings. Maybe you want to invest in physical and tangible assets - a remodeled shopping mall near your home or a new community center with interests you support.

With so many choices for financial growth, deciding on where to invest your money *and having the confidence to make sound decisions* are easily within your grasp.

I'm sure, at this point, it may seem challenging. You want to know all the ins and outs of where your dollars are going and also, the specifics on how those dollars will bring you wealth.

This is often the 'pain' of investing - trying to make investment decisions without having the know-how to make those investments *wisely*.

To make wise decisions, it is imperative to understand how each investment tool functions and the benefits and risks of each. With so many options, gaining this knowledge could take you years, something that, if you are reading this book, I'm fairly certain you aren't interested in.

If, however, you could confidently:

- Scan the horizon for opportunities without feeling lost;
- Choose the best opportunities from the many available; ones that fit your goals and timeline;
- Know exactly how your money is being invested and how it will grow;
- Be able to read between the lines to improve a deal, or walk away from a poor one; and
- Know what it will take in order for you to show substantial profits;

then you would confidently be able to do it over again and again and again.

I'm Michael Steven, and I've financed deals worth over $1 billion in real estate. I've helped people and families eliminate millions of dollars of debt, and have over 30 years of experience in the finance and investment industries. Currently, I am a mortgage director and real estate investor. I am married and have three boys, and I've been in your shoes.

I understand what it feels like to be under the control of something more powerful, unable to determine my own outcome. I wanted to be the 'boss' of my own financial security and future.

By having been where you are, I understand the frustration and the doubt you are feeling - like you'll never get out from underneath an established and broken system.

You can trust me when I say it is possible for you to achieve financial freedom without a lot of money.

What would having this insight and knowledge do for your lifestyle, right now?

How would it change your future?

Learning this process doesn't have to be time-consuming drudgery. The background 'nuts and bolts' of numerable investment strategies are, quite literally, at your fingertips. You can get the information you need to earn a great profit with one simple and sustainable strategy.

In *Commercial Real Estate: Journey Towards Financial Freedom*, not only will you have all your questions answered with easily understood terms and methods, but you will also find out about the important questions *you don't even know exist.*

- How would I invest in real estate without purchasing directly?
- Is there any difference between residential and CRE investing?
- Don't I need tens of thousands of dollars to invest in CRE?
- How long will I have to wait before I receive money back on my investments?

As you begin to see the advantages of CRE investing, you will understand how certain opportunities are favorable, while others can turn into a money pit within days.

You'll also gain knowledge of how to develop your own strategy and find the investment options which work best for you to help you achieve your goals. Being able to compare specific markets, past performance, and future development plans will give you an edge in making smart investments. This in turn, gives you the control to build your returns and enhance your future values based on your investment commitments.

There are several types of commercial property you can invest in, and the degree of involvement on your part can be high or low. Because there are many opportunities and people involved in CRE, from the developer and contractor to financial lenders, property managers, tenants, and maintenance agents, you'll learn how to spot the advantages and disadvantages of each opportunity. The weighing of details about what suits you best for your financial goals, and what you are hoping the investment will do for you, will become second nature as you navigate through properties and real estate deals. Soon, you'll wonder why you ever felt apprehensive and unsure.

Read through the chapters as they are written, beginning to end, and make sure you understand the concepts, terms and processes before moving on to the next.

You don't have to memorize them, just make sure you *understand them*. All terms are listed as the steps are explained, so referring back to the concepts is simple.

Also, because there are several ways to approach investing in CRE, don't feel you must know each one instinctively. As you read, get a feel for which ones appeal to you and will fit into your financial scope. You can always come back to your bookmarked sessions to further your knowledge in other specific areas.

Keep in mind, it will serve you well to know these processes and terms very well. There are many, so focus on the ones which interest you the most; they will serve you best as you begin. By doing this, you build confidence.

While you further your finesse, you will become more experienced and familiar with all the concepts and options for CRE. Many people make huge amounts of money with CRE alone in their portfolios, while others use it to diversify their portfolios. As you learn the basics and develop your techniques, you will discover which concepts work best for you. That is when the revenue will accumulate automatically.

Remember, don't feel you need to learn all of these concepts immediately. Take it slow, understand the process, focus in on the ideas which appeal to you, and be thorough in your execution. By taking in the broad picture and exploring your investment options from the beginning, you will develop solid building blocks and achieve growth and profits in no time. You'll also be more at ease with your own ability to change options, discuss terms, and sign deals.

Whether you are familiar with CRE investing, or have no notion of it at all, by reading this book and following my suggestions, you are starting off well. You'll find as you read, each detail is thoroughly explained, giving you the facts you'll need when outlining your strategy to build your way to financial freedom.

Most people feel they are fairly well versed when it comes to real estate investments. They have either purchased a home or condominium, or they know someone who has. CRE, however, has some exciting and unique twists to consider.

There are many different types of CRE properties - ice cream shops, doctor offices, boutique stores, apartment buildings, sports centers, and storage units, to just name a few.

Because there are so many different types of CRE property, there are just as many specialized and separate types of financing tools. These can get you where you want to be when purchasing, as well as be strategic ways to get there. Many people will also be on your team to advise you, network with you, partner with you, and be a hired hand.

All of these options are here for your benefit. Don't feel you have to use one or many. You don't even have to use any at all. The main idea here is that you know what's available to you, to not only help you determine the best and quickest way to begin making money, but also the smartest way to set things up so you continue to make money, tomorrow, and in the next 10, 20, and 30 years.

What does it mean to be a CRE investor?

- More opportunity to be successful
- Diverse options for investment

Yes, these things and so much more. This is a ride which will change your life!

Let's get started …

CHAPTER ONE: COMMERCIAL REAL ESTATE - HOW CAN I BENEFIT FROM WHAT IT HAS TO OFFER?

※※※

'Landlords grow rich in their sleep, without working, risking, or economizing.'

— *JOHN STUART MILL, POLITICAL ECONOMIST*

As the introduction stated, commercial real estate (CRE) investments can be a very lucrative way to build your wealth and give you financial independence. Learning the basics of CRE is essential. If you don't understand, and you try to take advantage of all the options CRE has to offer, you will be short-changing yourself and your financial future.

Whether you are building your first investment strategy or adding CRE to an already established financial portfolio, having money working for you in CRE will boost your profits in simple, recurring, and exponential ways.

The advantages of CRE ownership are numerous and can create a steady flow of profits in many ways. CRE's create steady cash flow, and if that isn't enough to catch your attention, they also have a future potential of increased income as the economic markets grow (increased rent and equity), providing consistent tenant occupancy and lowering vacancy risks.

If you have the financial backing to fund your own property purchases, you can also gain money with acquisition fees when closing your deal.

CRE property types:

- Apartment complexes which have 5 units or more
- Mobile home communities
- Office buildings
- Industrial parks
- Retail and shopping centers
- Special purpose properties (specific retail space such as fast-food restaurants or convenience stores)
- Self-storage facilities
- Hotels and motels
- Tenancy in common (TIC - joint ownership with other investors)
- Real Estate Investment Trust (REIT - trust investment with many properties)
- CRE owned properties (bank acquired foreclosures)
- Commercial short sales (negotiated upside down property acquisitions)
- Real estate crowdfunding (similar to REIT's, but property purchase is specific).

As you can see, it is almost easier to say what CRE property isn't than what it is. Most properties which aren't residential are considered commercial, and they are determined by the property's intent to make money. If it's rented out, creates investment profits, or fulfills a number of other criteria, it is determined to be CRE because it is *generating income*.

By knowing each opportunity inside and out, you will feel confident and assured your investment is a wise one. The process used to determine if a property will be a good investment is an easy one to learn. Once you've mastered the process, the key is *to be thorough*. One of the richest men in the world stated it best:

"Only invest in things you have an understanding of." - Warren Buffet

By understanding exactly what the details of your investment are, you are in control of the variables and you have determined the predictability of profit. Learning these basic rules, you will be able to see when it is a good idea to wait on an investment, when to move forward and purchase, when to sell a property, the criteria which makes having a partner profitable, and when to settle in with your investments for current growth.

These are not complicated practices, and rarely will you see successful investors veering from these practices.

Having control of your investment in CRE comes down to six key areas for success. They are:

1. *Money spent*: You are in control of the expenses of the property because you are ultimately signing the checks.
2. *Income*: By collecting rent, you also determine the amount of income you will be receiving.
3. *Property assets*: It is your choice whether to keep a property or sell it, or to refinance for other possible advantages.
4. *Insurance*: You purchase the level of coverage and type of insurance you want.

5. *Debt owing*: You are in charge of the financial arrangements.
6. *Property management*: Hiring property managers and staff is solely your choice.

Predictability of profit and growth are determined by criteria you will learn to gather and assess. Past performance and economy, future community planning and development, and current market sustainability, along with several other factors, will weigh into your final analysis and determination of a profitable opportunity.

When evaluating your investment options and weighing the risk with different investment vehicles, you'll quickly see how these advantages give you increased confidence and a greater advantage. By having more control and being able to base your predictable success ranking with such valued data, your risk quotient can be much less than with other financial opportunities, such as stocks or mutual funds.

Knowing these practices for determining and evaluating how you want to invest in CRE's greatly increases the possibility of owning highly successful properties. However, it is important to realize all investments do have risks. By decreasing this risk, you also decrease the likelihood of purchasing a poor investment. The bottom line is: know the key factors to look for in every CRE investment, weigh the past performance, assess the probable outcomes for the future, and determine if the investment will turn a profit.

INVESTMENT RETURNS

Not only do you make money from the rent paid by your tenants, but you will also gain property appreciation in the form of equity and property value. Due to the fact that you will most often have your tenants in a term lease, you can count on this bottom line as part of your cash flow and profits. Residential leases can run from months to a few years for apartment complexes, while business leases are generally written for longer periods of time; two to 10 years and beyond.

If you are thinking of applying for any kind of monetary support, the financial institution will need a background of rental receipts (or proposed values for new developments) as well as your suggested use for the property. We'll discuss the details of these practices later in the book, but for now, learning these basics will benefit you in the larger game plan.

Now that you have a fairly good idea of what CRE investing is and the basics of the properties and their characteristics, I want to discuss the advantages and disadvantages of investing in CRE.

As I see it, the advantages far outweigh the disadvantages, but not everyone is me. Because investing one's own money is such a personal and important choice, I want you to understand all the points which you'll be dealing with in the beginning, in addition to knowing about your future decisions and options. I've already mentioned some of them, so you'll see a couple repeated here. If they are repeated, it means they are *twice as important to understand.*

ADVANTAGES OF COMMERCIAL REAL ESTATE

- The lease contracts for business tenants are longer. You won't be writing a new lease every few months and you'll also be able to count on a steady cash flow.
- Attractive leasing rates make CRE investing a high yielding source of income, as well as being

consistent because they are backed by an agreement.
- There is a high potential for capital appreciation - real estate is one of the most stable collateral investments you can make.
- You can leverage CRE against a stock market-based portfolio, giving you more diversification and better overall performance of your investments.
- The volatility of CRE is low because the market moves slower in real estate. You also are able to anticipate trends when other securities wobble, giving you more time to evaluate and adjust your intentions.
- You have a distinct advantage against inflation with real estate and it's stability. Though CRE has been known to drop in value during economic downturns, generally the downturns are small in comparison to other investment options.
- Having more tenants in a CRE property helps mitigate the risk of non-paying tenants, easing the burden of defaults.
- Your investment in a 'hard' asset gives you value for the long-term or medium-term.
- There is less volatility in CRE, lessening risk, and providing portfolio confidence.
- There are many more opportunities with a wider variance of options for CRE investors than in residential real estate, or other investment opportunities.
- Tax benefits are numerous, including claim deductions on property improvements/catastrophes, depreciation, and loss

write-offs (which are not available on any other investment), expenses, and interest write-offs.

DISADVANTAGES OF COMMERCIAL REAL ESTATE

- You will be using more capital to invest in CRE since it is a bigger arena of opportunities with bigger commitments.
- Regulation restrictions are stricter in CRE than in residential. The regulations differ between municipalities – check the area when you are doing your research.
- The leases are written for lengthier terms, so commitment on your part is for longer periods of time. CRE is not a get in, get rich, and get out investment. You are dealing in long-term investing.
- Renovation upgrades and tenant requests for customized renovations are more expensive than residential and are non-existent for other investment vehicles. Changing facility build-outs as your tenants come and go can get pricey.
- Most often, the customizations and renovations will have to be done professionally.
- These investments are NOT considered as a liquid asset on financial statements.

At this point, if you are thinking you may want to *investigate residential real estate investment as opposed to commercial*, let's compare some facts for this scenario as well.

ADVANTAGES OF RESIDENTIAL OVER COMMERCIAL

- Initial investments are smaller, as are the final costs for investments.
- A house is easier to work on if renovations are needed, and they can be managed by yourself if you like.
- Lease terms are usually for less time, enabling you to raise rent amounts more frequently between tenants.
- There are fewer details to contend with.

DISADVANTAGES OF RESIDENTIAL OVER COMMERCIAL

- Rent and cash flow are less, and sometimes, can even go into the red if upgrades or catastrophes are substantial. Diversification of income streams is inherent in most commercial properties.
- Money used for down payments comes directly from the investor. No financial institutions are involved prior to the mortgage settlement.
- Financial options are considerably reduced and have higher liability.
- Tenants tend to be harder on your investment property, as they are living there full-time, as opposed to working at the property only during business hours.
- Lease terms are for less time, resulting in more paperwork to contend with, as well as needing to interview new tenants more often.
- Investors/owners are more financially dependent on one single-tenant, increasing the risk of default

on financing if a vacancy occurs often or is lengthy.
- Most residential investors tend to take on the duties of a property manager, creating more work and upkeep than is anticipated (or wanted!).

Now, I may have been biased in listing these facts, but in all the years I've been helping people reduce and eliminate debt, as well as build up their financial wealth for early retirement, I seldom give advice on acquiring residential real estate (aside from them owning their own home). In most cases before investing, there is a set of circumstances which is propelling my clients into wanting a secure future such as a new job, or a new lifestyle. Rarely do residential property investments result in massive wealth build-up.

There are some terms you will hear often as you read through this book. You should be very well-versed in the meaning and use of each of them and what they mean to your CRE investments. These terms are described below.

CASH FLOW

Understanding and managing your cash expectations is an essential part of success, and having a sizable cash flow (the excess of cash when subtracting the expenses from your income) will give you the cushion you will need when emergencies and unexpected costs arise.

While considering how you will attain a sizeable cash flow, consider these questions:

- What percentage of income-to-expenses is a good margin to have when considering a CRE opportunity?
- Can a higher-end CRE investment outweigh the

deficits of higher costs and upkeep, affecting the final cash flow margin?

You'll answer these questions and many more as you evaluate a property's value. Combined, these figures will help you decide if you have sufficient cash flow to maintain your investment as well as stay in line with your financial goals. When you have determined the amount of income you will need to maintain the property, pay all expenses, and support your own needs, then you will better be able to set parameters and compare the details of each option of purchase. After you have calculated these figures, you will have a clear picture of the potential cash flow of any particular investment and the potential revenue it will make for you, giving you a clear picture of whether it is a good investment for you or a poor one.

Keep in mind, one of the goals of investing in a CRE is to lessen the risks of loss while increasing the profit margin. A wise investment will check all the boxes you have previously outlined in a business plan and goal strategy. In CRE, there are more opportunities available for ideal investments, giving you a better chance of finding the perfect property.

VALUE ADD

A property which is deemed as a 'value add' property means it needs some kind of improvements to attain the levels of value appropriate to its location or stature. No matter what the necessary work is, the improvements must be made before it will be able to be rented to a tenant.

Perhaps it will need a full renovation. Maybe the zoning for the area has changed and it needs upgrades to comply with them. Other criteria could involve landscaping improvements, while still another may involve handicap access requirements.

Consider intense inspections for these types of properties and make sure you know exactly what you are purchasing before following through with such an investment. This is sound advice for any real estate purchase, but when a property is listed as 'value add', line up your team to make sure all issues are noted and understood before you buy it.

Another consideration with 'value add' properties is that once you have made the improvements, you will be able to capitalize on your investments immediately, without having to wait for equity to grow or values to increase. You will have created your own value increase and will be able to see it when the property is ready to rent. This will not only increase your cash flow but will result in a higher value when you decide to sell the property.

HOLDING TIME

This is the time between the purchase of the property and the time you are able to have it occupied by renters. If you purchased a property which is ready to rent or already has occupied spaces, you have no holding time. If you purchased a 'value add' property, depending on the time it will take to complete the needed improvements, the holding time could be anywhere from 1 to 3 years (average holding time of CRE's).

If you were to make the renovations and then sell before occupying the property, this is known as a 'flipping' strategy, whereas what we have been talking about as an investment strategy is known as a 'buy and hold' strategy. The higher the appreciation for an area, the more likely it has a dominantly 'buy and hold' CRE market.

APPRECIATION

Though CRE investments are generally purchased to stabilize a financial portfolio and provide passive income (money earned by other means than an hourly wage), some may purchase CRE properties to hold onto them for a smaller amount of time and cash in on the appreciation gained from purchase to sale dates. Some factors which may cause you to rethink an investment which was otherwise intended as a long-term investment are:

- The property is in need of substantial improvements which may deem it a costly investment, and selling it would be the most beneficial outcome.
- The area has been re-zoned by the municipalities and the required improvements or changes have become undesirable for you.
- The market has increased to the point that selling would make you more money than the current rental situation.
- The property has become a burden instead of an asset.

These situations do arise and can contribute, over time, to your overall assessment of a CRE in your financial strategy. When we dig further into assessing properties, you will see how each one of these points can affect your bottom line investment value.

Before moving on, let's dig a bit deeper into leasing and the many financial instrument options.

There are more creative ways to purchase CRE than there are stars in the skies. Okay, maybe not that many, but there certainly are more options available than a residential property investment can offer. The most important one is that you don't need to invest your own money into the purchase.

If you don't have the cash up-front for a down payment, there are many other options which can be used to acquire the investment property. Several types of leases are available for varied levels of investment and involvement in your property.

COMMERCIAL LEASE OPTIONS

We talked a bit about tenant leases, but let's take a closer look at what is available and which lease(s) may work the best for your situation.

Gross lease: The tenant pays only for rent. The property taxes, insurance, and maintenance of the property are covered by the landlord/owner.

Single-net lease: This lease type is very popular for investors, as it places the burden of increased property taxes on the tenant, in addition to the rent, utilities, and any additional fees of the tenant. These types of leases also lock you into a term (usually ten years or so), but for many on both sides of the lease, it is a viable and lucrative lease option.

Double-net (NN) lease: With this lease type, the tenant is responsible for the property tax payments as well as the insurance, in addition to the rent and fees. If you opt for this kind of lease, make sure the insurance is acceptable for your property coverage needs.

Triple-net (NNN) lease: The tenant is responsible for paying the property taxes, insurance, and maintenance of the property, in addition to the agreed-upon rent and fees. This leaves the owner/landlord free and clear of any fluctuating costs or management of the property, aside from collecting the rent. This is a very lucrative option for the investor, as it requires the investor to spend less money, lessening the burden and sharing the risk with the tenant, as well as distancing the owner's involvement in day-to-day management.

We will examine these lease options in further detail later in the book, so you will get a full picture of the benefits of each, and how they can be advantageous in certain situations.

INTEREST RATES

As with any monetary lending tool, the interest rate for commercial properties is based on the current prime rate. These rates differ per institution, depending on their need to sign loans and factors unique to each institution.

The prime rate is the lowest possible rate at which money can be lent commercially.

The bank borrows money at the prime rate, then adds the necessary interest percentages to make the loan feasible for them to lend, and offers this tallied rate to you, the borrower. The bank makes its money from the difference between the prime rate and what they are charging you.

AMORTIZATION

The amortization period is the length of time it will take to pay the loan off. It can be adjusted to allow longer periods of time to pay off the debt. This will increase the interest rate, but the debt payment each month is lower. By comparison, a shorter amortization period results in lower interest rates and overall interest paid, but it also has higher payments each month.

When you finance a loan, you will receive an amortization schedule which has all of your payments listed and how they are paid to the principal, interest, and other possible fees which may be included in the loan. Most commercial loans have a longer amortization period and are often based on the cash flow of the property instead of the appraised value.

Another document you will want to be familiar with is the *Commercial Rental Property Proforma*. This is basically the financial analysis of the property as it exists currently, or how it is projected to perform. A good Property Proforma will include:

- Base rental income of the property (proving tenants are paying market rates).
- Vacancy loss, representing the lost income which occurs between tenant leases. This is considered a loss of potential revenue instead of an expense.
- Concessions, or incentives, which may be offered to new tenants to entice them to rent. Most often, it is a reduction in rent for a limited period of time.
- Credit loss or bad debt, a projection of the non-paid rent, and other forms of loss of revenue. Generally, it is projected at 2% of the expected gross income.
- Expense reimbursements are the expenses each tenant is responsible for, including property taxes, insurance, and utilities, though it can vary with each lease agreement.

The total of all the items listed above will give you the net worth of revenue the property is projected to generate. Additional items to add to this basic list are:

- Application fees.
- Cleaning and damage fees.
- Late fees.

- NSF charges.

Next, the Proforma will list the expenses of the property, which consist of:

- Operating expenses, including maintenance, repairs, utilities, and contingency fund savings.
- Property management fees if there are any agencies who oversee the property and its amenities.
- Real estate and property taxes.

GROSS REVENUE

This is the total amount of revenue received from the commercial property if 100% of all units are occupied with paying tenants.

VACANCY

Most often, this is a percentage of the gross revenue. It is based on the current occupied rate, less 5%.

OPERATING EXPENSES

This is the total figure of combined operating expenses of the property. This would include property taxes, management fees, insurance, utilities, and any maintenance fees.

DEBT SERVICE

Any proforma document will have this included and it is in reference to the debt (or loan) payment. It excludes operating expenses.

GROSS OPERATING INCOME (GOI)

All investors rely on this figure to tell them what it will cost to run their property. This number considers estimated tenant vacancies and credits from potential operating income. It gives you the bottom line about the potential operating income for the property.

NET OPERATING INCOME (NOI)

This is the total value of cash remaining after all expenses to run the property are paid, but before paying taxes. Income can include rent, parking fees, or monthly assessed costs to tenants. Expenses can also include vacancy, credit losses, insurance, management fees, utilities, and maintenance expenses (including legal and accounting retainers). The formula for calculating this figure is:

NOI = Gross Revenue − Vacancy − Operating Expenses

Cap Rate

This is the net operating income written in percentage form in comparison to the amount paid for the commercial investment property. It is generated before the value of debt service is taken out, or paid. In simple terms, this figure estimates your potential return of revenue on a property. You'll be using this figure routinely when comparing properties. Naturally, when Cap Rates go up, the return on your investment goes down.

CASH-ON-CASH (COC) OR CASH YIELD

The COC is your return on investment (ROI) after you have paid your debt-service costs. This figure is not based on the purchase price of your property, it is based on the investment amount (down payment) you initially made when you purchased the property, and measures the investment performance (the revenue your property is bringing in to you).

INTERNAL RATE OF RETURN (IRR)

An IRR will show how your investment is performing. It is calculated as a *comparison* of how your property is actually performing compared to surrounding businesses in the area. It is similar to a utility bill which compares your consumption to your neighbors. With this figure, you can see where improvements can be made or where your investment is really making a difference in your revenue.

CHAPTER SUMMARY

- By using CRE as an investment tool, you have a high potential of making a profitable investment using basic tools and calculations.
- CRE is more expensive initially, but the returns are higher and the investment is able to withstand economic fluctuations better than residential real estate investments.

In the next chapter, you will see how solidifying a sound foundation of knowledge can benefit your investment strategy, even in the 'unpredictable' year of 2020.

CHAPTER TWO: PLANNING YOUR STRATEGY FOR COMMERCIAL REAL ESTATE INVESTING

❈❈❈

Almost every industry and business has experienced a major development event in recent years, and commercial real estate (CRE) investing is no different. These facts, as we'll discuss here, can benefit you if you know how to identify the ideal circumstances for maximizing your own financial standing and portfolio goals.

Though the year 2020 brought numerous emotional and physical changes, it has also brought advantages to investors, particularly if you analyze a few innovative angles and choose to think outside the box. It has weeded out poor investment options and weak opportunities backed with shallow funding, making way for stronger-valued investments, which in turn, show longer-term profits.

Tenant needs are also changing. If you are thinking of a CRE investment in multiple rental units, many tenants will be looking for extra space, in order to work remotely or homeschool their children. If you are leaning towards industrial ventures, square footage has been somewhat reduced. This trend has been decreasing in many industries, as technology has reduced the need for space and amenities considerably.

Tenants are also becoming more aware of their environmental footprint, preferring their spaces to have less impact on the environment.

Renters of home units are also moving towards the preferences of living in a place which has 'smart technology', and they are willing to pay the extra rent costs for it. Along with these desires, renters are also hoping to have convenience in their communities. Walking distance to entertainment, groceries, and activities play a huge role for up-and-coming generations. They might also value scooter or electric bicycle options for transportation.

Tenants are looking for simpler lives which give them flexibility and options. A wise investor will take these views into consideration when evaluating the purchase of a property.

There are also emerging commercial markets which are developing into progressive and appealing communities due to the increasing job opportunities from growing markets. These include Scottsdale, AZ, Austin, TX, Columbia, MD, Colorado Springs, CO, Raleigh, NC, Boston, MA, and Orlando, FL. Investment projects are also emerging in these, and many more cities, supporting the millennials and their focus on sustainability, convenience, and lifestyle.

When considering CRE options, don't limit yourself to established buildings only. Investing in land, development opportunities, and prospective group investment vehicles can also offer great prospects for profit while asking for less investment dollars.

Are you feeling a bit overwhelmed?

It is at this point, rather than feeling like you need to know it all in order to make a wise decision, that you need to realize there are hundreds of thousands of millions of opportunities to participate in. There are good ones and there are bad ones. There are also opportunities which may be a good choice for one person, yet a bad choice for another.

How do you differentiate between the good and the bad?

How do you decide on what investment to pursue and what investment to walk away from? *Analyze!*

If you aren't willing to do your homework and research, then you won't be able to achieve success in the CRE investment arena.

In order to set goals, plot a beginning path, focus on specifics, and be willing to adjust your sights when adverse conditions arise since you will need to take initiatives. There is a difference between taking initiative and making a rash financial decision. Set criteria when creating the financial structure of what a good investment would look like for you.

What kind of investment options work best with your current situation?

- Weigh different CRE investment options when considering your investment criteria.
- Set goals and respect the patience you will need to keep them in sight.
- Develop a resistance to being emotionally swayed when analyzing an investment.

Now that you understand the basics of what it will take in order to get to where you want to be, namely financial freedom, let's discuss a few of the many choices of CRE you have for investing in.

Industrial real estate: This includes warehouse, manufacturing facilities, refrigeration buildings, storage units, and business data centers.

Apartment real estate: These buildings need to have at least 5 apartments or more to be considered CRE.

Retail real estate: Included in retail real estate are single-unit properties, small 'strip mall' interests, and multi-anchor store development complexes with multiple store access and community development (movie theaters, bowling alleys, etc.).

Office buildings: This ranges from a small office building with several units to multiple level office developments.

Due to the fact that CRE investing involves large bankrolls, financing options have grown in creative, beneficial ways for developers and investors alike. This makes it easy for individuals to invest in small and large investment opportunities, no matter the 'buy in' cost. Crowdsourcing partnerships and group investors are becoming more and more prevalent. This offers more people a greater opportunity to become involved in the ever-growing and changing investment vehicle of CRE.

What does this mean for you?

When considering a CRE purchase, not only can you invest in a property alone, but you can also invest with a group of like-minded people to give everyone more buying power. Your own financial limitations may only allow you to invest $2,000. If you couldn't find a property which satisfied your criteria for a possible purchase, an investment opportunity with others who are like-minded could be a good option for you. Some of these special opportunities have a buy-in of as little as $100.

These types of opportunities give you more choice of investments that exactly fit your needs and revenue structure. The time couldn't be better for investors to profit.

So you can better understand each type of CRE asset, I want to give you a more detailed version of each property description. Along with this, you'll notice some specific benefits which may be possible to attain with each asset. Keep in mind, these are things to be aware of if you are looking at a particular type of property and they will, most often, change depending on the location and economic structure of the property.

INDUSTRIAL

These properties are often manufacturing, storage or maintenance spaces, often offering property customized with machinery, shipping and receiving docks, and heavy-duty structural components. They might meet location needs, such as proximity to natural resources such as water, or they might be near a major highway. These are the most common types of CRE properties sought for investment, as the costs and potential returns for these properties are often favorable.

OFFICE

Office space can give you many options for investing, including offices adjacent to a retail area, a two-level building with several offices within it, a group of small buildings, a consulting company or private practice specialists. Because this type of real estate asset is so large, they are categorized into different classes. They are:

Class A: More often than not, these properties are newly built or extensively renovated structures, with ideal access to popular amenities and community. They are managed by real estate management companies for the investors who purchased them.

Class B: These buildings usually require some minor

updates after purchase, or a bit of investment capital to bring it up to optimal rental value. Some type of repair and upgrade can be expected, which makes them a desirable investment, as the price is usually lower and set for an optimal turnaround, yet the property is in good condition and in desirable locations.

Class C: Buildings in this class are usually priced for redevelopment. They are often in older communities and in need of major renovations or improvements, either to the buildings themselves, the areas they are located in, or both. Infrastructure may also be dated or need to be brought up to code (think earthquake restructure or electrical code updates) and have a lower occupancy rate than higher classed buildings. If there is money to upgrade the structures as needed, these can be very lucrative investments, generally positioned for an astute investor or developer who is well informed in building renovations.

RETAIL

Retail real estate properties include stores and strip malls, banks, restaurants, and service centers. Most often, you'll find these properties in urban areas, and they range from 3,000 square feet to over 350,000 square feet in size.

MULTIFAMILY

Though most often thought of as duplexes and smaller rental buildings, high-rise condominium buildings and multiple family estates can be grouped into this asset type as well. Rental rates are usually less per unit, but due to the larger volume of tenants, there is a somewhat stable revenue source. Low vacancy rates are important to success, due to this fact. Tenant turnover should be a consideration, as optimal loan criteria is usually based on a 60% occupancy rate. Lease terms are usually less than industrial or retail commercial property.

SPECIAL PURPOSE

Properties that are considered 'special purpose' have specific characteristics which make them difficult to repurpose into other types of space - consider a car wash, public civic center, or storage facilities as good examples. They can be small endeavors or large, including hotels, sports stadiums, and amusement parks.

ADDITIONAL NOTE

There is a new CRE option which has been rising to the top of many investors lists and it is worth adding to our list. These are the up-and-coming 'mixed-use' developments. They are mini-communities of their own and usually combine many different living opportunities for the public and commercial opportunities for private sector businesses. As an example, picture an apartment building with retail stores on the street level, or a gated community built on a private beach with separate living units, a small restaurant, health center, and boutique market. Mixed-use developments continue to grow in popularity for age-specific communities, as well as for people with unique lifestyle preferences.

Another term you will come across is OOCRE or owner-occupied commercial real estate. This is when the investor(s) is investing in real estate with the intent of utilizing it for their own purposes. It can be used in any CRE property investment mentioned above, and is an ideal option for those who want to have a 'hands-on' experience with their investment and business opportunity.

Now you have a very good idea of what is considered CRE, some of the generalities which are involved with each type of asset investment, and an idea of the commitment level each entails or can offer.

You've probably realized tenant personas play an important part in what kind of CRE you're interested in, whether you want to be involved directly with the process or hire a management group to govern your tenants and their leases. As you most likely have realized, governing an apartment building with over 100 units will be much different than writing up the leases for a small strip mall of 5 separate retail units.

A FEW MORE CONSIDERATIONS …

If you haven't thought of this before, consider the location of your property and how that will attract tenants. For example, investing in a restaurant will have a much better chance of being profitable if it is located close to urban centers and popular destinations than in a mostly residential area.

As you've read through the descriptions, inevitably you've decided which ones you would consider in your investments, which ones you would definitely not be a part of, and the possible choices you feel have great potential down the road, once you are a bit more experienced and confident in your investing.

BENEFITS FOR YOU, THE INVESTOR …

When you choose to invest in CRE, you are entering a 'business' world, filled with more opportunities to meet people who are interested in the same ideas you are. Business-to-business (B2B) relationships develop quicker when you have a common interest, and finding future opportunities will come easier and with less work when you get in with your own 'niche' of real estate investors in your area. You will also find, by developing and engaging in the relationships you have with your business tenants, you can expand your business community and business network. Who doesn't like to grow?! It is a critical part of most successful businesses.

You will also be able to conduct business during business hours. Since your tenants will be businesses, they will generally keep 'business hours' and won't have needs which reach outside the workweek. Of course, this is different for residential apartment properties which often have 24-hour tenant needs, with evenings and weekends being a common time for tenants to want to address issues.

For the most part though, you won't be getting a call at 4 a.m. telling you the sink is clogged if you are focussed on business properties, or larger apartment buildings which are managed by a third-party.

So, we've determined that even though the costs of investment are higher, you can leverage those costs with the knowledge that:

- You won't lose your personal property if you experience a loss (if you set up your business as an LLC).
- The chances of making a higher revenue are almost double that of residential investments.
- Choices for opportunities have a broad range, meaning you can invest in something you are excited about.

- Tenant leases are longer, resulting in a more lucrative cash flow and less paperwork.
- Business opportunities are increased by networking and industry relationships.
- And the best part of all…
- You Can Make Great Money!

Sound good?

Great, it's time to start making your plan…

YOUR FIRST STEPS

The first and foremost idea to understand and live by is this: *You need to do your homework.*

If you aren't willing to research properties, compare numbers, and analyze the markets with tried and true calculators and methods, you won't make good business decisions and you won't make any money in CRE investing. There are rules to abide by and applying them to each possible property purchase can be the difference in making a wise and profitable business decision or falling victim to chance and circumstance.

Begin with these basics:

1. *Know the CRE business inside and out.* Know why CRE is different from other real estate properties. The relevance of square footage is more important than in residential properties, simply because the rental value is compared on broader terms. Locale also plays an important part in the value, and again, your analysis of this factor will contribute greatly to the bottom line of it being a good investment or not. Along with this fact is the need

to understand your tenants' relationship to the location of the property. If the property is in a well-populated area, you'll be looking for a tenant with the need for foot-traffic, or if the office is set apart in a quiet neighborhood, perhaps consultants or therapists would benefit from your location. Know who you will be offering your property to and if it's a viable location for their business.

2. *Surround yourself with knowledgeable and experienced people who have been in their field for a reasonable amount of time and have a successful business record.* Liken this rule to having an experienced mechanic for your expensive automobile. You wouldn't have just anyone change out the suspension on your BMW, would you? Apply the same dedication and diligence to your business and choose a team for your investment inquiries and financing. By hiring a few key players to work with you on real estate inquiries and financial options, you will reap many rewards. Initially, you may pay a few dollars upfront, but in the long run, these expenses will pay for themselves in time and investment. If chosen with care, you can surround yourself with realtors, agents, legal counsel, and financial experts who not only know how to do their job well, but they will put those years of knowledge to work for you, so you will both be successful and look forward to making more profitable investments together in the future.

3. *Compare the value of the offer to what has sold recently.* This is where your research will pay off greatly. By finding comparable properties and seeing their pricing, you can see if your investment is priced

well, or if it offers other benefits that tenants might consider. If it's priced high, determine why the cost is higher. Does it have tenants currently who are bound to a lease? Are there extra customized amenities which may make it tough to find tenants in the future since only a few types of businesses would need them? Generally, you'll want to stay within 10% of the price you are contemplating. Unless you can determine exactly the pros and cons of a property and judge it to be worthy (without emotion!), you may want to rethink the investment.

4. *Make sure you know your financing forwards and backwards.* Having a realistic perception of what is available to you and what isn't is the best way to make the most money on your investments. By arming yourself with every detail possible, you'll know how to make an okay deal a great one, or you'll know to walk away from something which looks good initially but has huge problems revealed after you dig deeper. Refer to the terms we discussed in the first chapter.

5. *Lessen the risk of your investment.* This is a rule you're going to abide by as much as you can, but the difference between doing just a little investigating and knowing you have done everything possible to avoid losing money, will be the difference between success and defeat. Add to that the avoidance of common investment mistakes, and you'll be well on your way to making money right from the start.

6. You have to be diligent and thorough in every step of determining a property's value. When you

understand that each property has its own individual assets and issues, you will avoid the pitfalls of loss and ruin. Don't think any factor is a common denominator for a good or bad property. Only by getting all the details in place before the time of purchase and running the figures individually, will you benefit from a good decision and make a long-term profit.
7. Just because you know the ins and outs of purchasing a home doesn't mean you can jump into CRE and master an investment from start to finish. Two very important investment ideologies to understand, as well as master, are Loan-to-Value (LTV) and Debt-Service Coverage Ratio (DSCR). By understanding these concepts inside and out, you will be on your way to CRE investment savvy.
8. Remember Warren Buffet's quote from earlier in the book: *"Only invest in things you have an understanding of."* Truer words were never said, especially in relation to CRE investing. If you don't quite understand the offer, or there are a few items which are unclear, *DO NOT* move forward with the purchase. It is much better to miss out on an opportunity than it is to purchase a bad one. There will always be great deals for you, provided you keep your analysis thorough and are absolutely 100% sure of every item in the property description and purchase agreement.

CALCULATORS

Below are 10 real estate calculations you should know. By knowing these formulas and testing your numbers to your own CRE parameters, you'll be able to make great investment purchases.

If you're a bit intimidated by the formulas, don't worry, I provide links to my site, and there you will find online calculators. All you have to do is gather the numbers and insert them into the correct fields. Look through these formulas, however, to see why they are important and how they impact your analysis of a property.

Mortgage Payment: The formula used to calculate mortgage payments is quite complicated as it requires multiple variables, such as home price, down payment, loan term, and interest rate. In addition, the variables are expressed in months, so you need to convert the interest rate and loan term before calculating the formula.

To calculate a mortgage payment, you will need the loan principal, loan term, and the interest rate.

$$\text{Mortgage Payment} = P \; \frac{r(1+r)^n}{(1+r)^n - 1}$$

Where:

P is the loan principal

r is the monthly interest rate (APR divided by 12)

n is the number of monthly payments (loan term multiplied by 12)

Sample:

Loan principal (P): $200,000

Monthly Interest Rate (r): 0.0033 (4% APR divided by 12 months)

Number of monthly payments (n): 360 (number of months in 30 years)

It looks like this:

$$= \$200{,}000 \times \frac{0.0033(1+0.0033)^{360}}{(1+0.0033)^{360}-1}$$

$$= \$200{,}000 \times \frac{0.012}{2.274}$$

$$= \$200{,}000 \times 0.005$$

$$= \$1{,}000 \text{ monthly mortgage payment}$$

Capitalization Rate: The capitalization rate helps investors to evaluate the net income produced by a property, relative to its total purchase price. Because the cap rate also factors in vacancy rates and operating expenses, it is favored by the investment community as one of the most accurate methods of comparing similar income properties.

The capitalization rate helps evaluate the net operating income (CI) produced by an income property, relative to its total purchase price.

Capitalization Rate = (Net Operating Income / Total Property Price) X 100%

Sample:
NOI: $30,000
Total Property Price (Purchase Price plus additional rehab costs): $500,000
$30,000 / $500,000 = 0.06
0.06 X 100% = 6% Capitalization Rate

Rent Cost Ratio: The rent-to-cost ratio is a helpful tool for quickly comparing income values between similar properties in a given area. The cost in this case is the total investment cost for a property, including the cost of repairs and renovations. Investors should target properties with a rent-to-cost ratio above 1%, and then make sure to perform more in-depth cost-benefit analyses.

The rent to cost ratio is a helpful tool for quickly comparing income values between similar properties in a given area.

Rent Cost Ratio = (Monthly Rental Income / Total Property Price) X 100%

Sample:
 Monthly Rental Income: $2,000
 Total Property Price (Purchase Price, plus additional rehab costs): $250,000
 $2,000 / $250,000 = 0.008
 0.008 X 100% = 0.8% Rent Cost Ratio

Gross Yield: The gross rental yield provides investors with an idea of how much income a property generates, relative to its total purchase price. Shown as a percentage, a higher rental yield signifies a better investment. Gross yields are especially helpful when conducting income property market research. Investors can first target regions or zip codes with a strong average gross yield rate to help narrow down their property search.

The gross rental yield provides investors with an idea of

how much income a property generates, relative to its total purchase price.

$$\text{Gross Yield} = (\text{Annual Rental Income} / \text{Total Property Price}) \times 100\%$$

Sample:
Annual Rental Income: $24,000
Total Property Price (Purchase price plus additional rehab costs): $250,000
$24,000 / $250,000 = 0.096
0.096 X 100% = 9.6% Gross Yield

DEBT SERVICE RATIO: Financial institutions will closely examine a property's debt service ratio before financing a deal. Properties with a debt service ratio under 1.0 will lose money each month, so investors should pay close attention to this number. The calculation requires the annual debt service amount, which is the value of payments to be made on a loan over 12 months, including interest payments.

Lenders will refuse to finance a property with a debt service ratio under 1.0, which indicates the purchase will lose money each month.

$$\text{Debt Service Ratio} = (\text{Net Operating Income} / \text{Annual Debt Service})$$

Sample:
Net Operating Income (NOI): $30,000
Annual Debt Service: $25,000
$30,000 / $25,000 = 1.2 Debt Service Ratio

Cash-On-Cash Return: Investors tend to pay keen attention to cash-on-cash return because it calculates exactly how much of their investment they will earn back (in cash) in one year. This calculation not only helps to compare the profitability of investments, but can also help investors to decide what debt or equity structure to employ when financing the deal.

Cash-on-cash return tells investors exactly how much of their investment they have earned back, in cash, on an annual basis.

Cash-On-Cash Return = (Annual Cash Flow / Cash Outlay) X 100%

Sample:
Annual Cash Flow (Net Operating Income - Annual Debt Service: $5,000
Cash Outlay: $50,000
$5,000 / $50,000 = 0.1
0.1 X 100% = 10% Cash-On-Cash Return

THE 50% Rule: The 50% rule is good for coming up with a rough estimate of how much operating expenses for a rental or commercial property should be relative to the operating income, which includes the age, condition, and grade of the property. If a property's operating expenses exceed 50%, it is best to walk away from the deal.

Probable Operating Expenses = Operating Income X 50%

Sample:
   Operating Income: $50,000
   $50,000 X 0.5 = $25,000 Probable Operating Expenses

AFTER REPAIR VALUE (ARV): Calculating a property's after repair value (ARV) comes in handy for investors who want to know a property's projected value after renovations are made. It should be noted that the renovation value will often exceed the actual cost of making the renovations.

After Repair Value = Property Purchase Price + Renovation Value

Sample:
   Property Purchase Price: $250,000
   Renovation Value: $100,000
   $250,000 + $100,000 = $350,000 After Repair Value (ARV)

70% of ARV Rule: 70% of ARV is an important rule-of-thumb for investors to remember, as it helps create a guideline for coming up with a maximum bid price on a rehab property. In general, the maximum offer should be roughly 70% of the projected ARV, minus estimated repair costs. The purpose of the 70% rule is to help investors create a safety buffer to ensure that they can retain 30% of the earnings, as well as provide a cushion in case the rehab turns out to be more costly than originally estimated.

This number helps investors set a maximum offer for a rehab property at 70% of the after repair value, accounting for repair costs, so that roughly 30% of the expected return can be retained.

$$\text{Maximum Offer Price} = (\text{After Repair Value} \times 70\%) - \text{Estimated Repair Costs}$$

Sample:
 After Repair Value: $350,000
 Estimated Repair Cost: $50,000
 ($350,000 X 0.7) - $50,000 = $195,000

SQUARE FOOTAGE: Correctly adding up the square footage has a great impact on what sellers can set as the asking price for a property. Simply get out a tape measure, make a list of the dimensions in each qualifying finished space of property (qualifying areas state the average person must be able to stand up comfortably, 8 feet is a general rule), and then add up all the finished space totals to get the total property square footage.

$$\text{Square Footage} = \text{Length} + \text{Width}$$

Sample:
 Length: 20 feet
 Width: 15 feet
 20 feet X 15 feet = 300 square feet

KEY POINTS

As you begin to familiarize yourself with these calculations and start committing them to memory, there are also a few key points to help you keep these numbers straight and not get them mixed up as you learn.

When evaluating a property and comparing it to others you will have obtained for possible purchase or comparisons, keep these suggestions in mind.

- *Collect as much information as possible on similar features for each property you want to compare.* By making sure you are collecting the same type of information on each property, such as square footage, area location, number of bedrooms and bathrooms, and kitchen upgrades, you will have a balanced comparison, rather than having to discern separate amenities and trying to value them individually with each property. Think of it like the old adage 'comparing apples to apples'. Any other way only adds to your list of random facts and this becomes confusing and problematic.
- *Make sure you use the same calculations each time, with every property.* By keeping to the same regime for determining a property's value, costs, etc., and making sure you stick to the same process, you are again able to compare "like with like". By using one metric with one property, but trying another metric with another, you will have multiple property calculations, with all of them being useless for your purpose of rating each property and making comparisons.
- *Estimate property expenses with the dexterity of a surgeon.* There are so many variables which depend

on this figure being as close to the actual cost as possible. You may as well not even run any figures if you are going to estimate this figure casually and with little analysis. Due to the importance of this figure in calculations such as your net operating income, rental yield, and capitalization rates, having this expense figure can make a bad deal look good, causing you incremental damage and loss down the road. If you aren't confident about your numbers and analysis, contact local property management companies or rental landlords to see if your numbers line up with their expenses for similar properties.

- *Formulate your own boundaries and guidelines for each investment, and stick with them.* We've talked about this before, but it can't be said often enough. Don't let emotions govern your outcomes. By making sure each transaction is valued on its factual merit alone, you are more likely to make wise investments than poor ones. Another advantage will also come to light when you do this - setting your own boundaries gives you continuity, so as you become more familiar with running calculations and comparisons, so shall your process become more streamlined and proficient as you increase your knowledge with repetition and success.
- *Use tools and technology to help you whenever you can.* When you have a team of accountants, legal advisors, and financial backers, they help you determine the best possible way to invest your money. A toolbox of well-known technology and apps can also give you the security of having the best options at your disposal. Spreadsheets, online

tools, calculators, and estimators can give you extended information, organize your data, and identify profitable deals in a quick and easy fashion. By using these tools, you will also lessen the chance of incorrect data input and, dare we admit, human error. Many will only cost you the time of initial set up, leaving you to enter the figures once with each property and then it will calculate the final figures for you.

- *Use a real estate broker who is experienced in CRE.* The knowledge, experience, and access a broker can give you is priceless. Having a broker on your team will give you listings which reflect your ideal properties and give you valuable information on market and property uniqueness. They can connect you with contractors, legal agencies, engineers, loan officers, building inspectors, and any other professional you feel necessary for your support team. Find one who is specialized to your needs, and make sure their background is solid and their reputation is stellar. Ask for references and talk to past clients. Also, make sure you understand how they will list any property you will rent (or sell in the future), to make sure it will be promoted in the best way possible.

CHAPTER SUMMARY

- The better you know the calculations needed to evaluate a property, the easier it will be to make wise decisions about property purchases.
- Forming a team to help you navigate the finer

points of CRE will give you the edge you'll need to make successful purchases.

In the next chapter, you will learn how to analyze the location and market value of a property, using proven methods of comparison.

CHAPTER THREE: STEP ONE, PART ONE - STUDY THE MARKET

❊❊❊

By now, you have realized investing in commercial real estate (CRE) can be an involved and time-consuming process. Hopefully, you've also realized once you get the basics down, it will be an exciting and worthwhile venture to learn and become an expert in. It truly does get easier the more you do it.

When you consider the benefits of its consistent returns, growth potential, and passive income, the reality of becoming financially free by investing in CRE becomes more attainable with each new mastered concept.

As you probably suspect, not all properties are good investments, and it isn't just because they don't match your criteria or are out of your financial reach.

When considering properties and what type of investment you would like to evaluate for your portfolio, it is important - *very important* - to make sure you have all the details and facts you can possibly get your hands on.

Consider this example...

You've found a great property for a potential tenant. In fact, the building could be perfect, matching exactly what your client is looking for to open a bakery. The price is right too, and you can come up with the entire down payment yourself, giving you an edge by being able to charge an acquisition fee at closing. The rent you'll be able to get will be enough over your operating expenses to tuck a nice little something away for your next purchase, which now looks more likely to be sooner than you had anticipated.

Yes, everything seems to be lining up, except that the actual numbers don't quite add up. You ran the numbers and they look good, but there are four years in the history of this building which are undisclosed, and when it went up for sale the following year, it was for $50,000 less than it appraised for previously.

So, what do you do? Everything else seems to line up. Even the building inspector passed it, but what about those four years? What could have happened during that time which would have made such a big difference in the value?

Lots of things can happen to a property, especially in CRE. The land could have been flooded, creating extended damage. Or, perhaps the owner couldn't pay the loan, and it became abandoned, and the financial institution holding the loan didn't move on it for a considerable amount of time, which resulted in property dilapidation. Maybe the gas line broke and tenants had to be evacuated, and the owner couldn't bring the building up to code. Or, maybe the neighborhood had a zoning issue with CRE during those years.

A multitude of things could have happened. Some of them wouldn't affect the stability of the property or building. Yet, some of them could be very devastating. Then again, some owners might present it for sale with just a band-aid fix in place, so they can unload it quickly.

These are the times when it is most important to stand by your original, pre-set boundaries and make sure all the property's details are in order and accounted for. Perhaps the problem is something which you would be happy to contend with and solve. It could even give you a fair reason to lower the bid for purchase, but until you know exactly what you are dealing with, it's wise to step back, or even away from the deal. Another deal will always come along.

These are common facts - it is better to be safe and step away from possible future hardship than to purchase something which causes loss and adversity down the road.

Having all the answers to *when, what,* and *how* as you research a potential CRE property will mean the difference between success and failure.

Now that you realize the importance of getting all the answers to your questions, how do you make sure which property you consider is a good choice?

NOT ALL PROPERTY OPTIONS GIVE YOU HIGH REVENUE - CONSISTENCY IS A GOOD CHOICE

Because there are so many types of CRE, the profitability can vary greatly between each type. Not only are there the basic five types we've talked about - office, retail, multifamily, industrial, and special purpose - but consider the other types of CRE which fall under these broad classifications and offer incredible investment potential - self-storage units, senior-care facilities, hotels or motels, and land.

The economy plays a huge part in the variability of the returns you can attain from these types of properties. So can, as we have witnessed recently, a health crisis or economic upheaval. Some types of properties can skyrocket in demand, while others can fall into dormancy for months on end. Remember, investing in consistently well-thought-out investments builds your wealth in a steady and reliable fashion.

As a result, you should follow sound advice such as I've outlined below.

1. Determine the performance of each asset class in the current economy, making sure you have a clear idea of that sector's ability to show profit.

Because each market has its own personality as far as loss or profitability, it is important to understand that specific geographic areas vary greatly and all are unique to their own market saturation of supply and demand.

Researching the market supply in the property's area is essential. Compare the current rentable square footage including renovations or changes you would make to the property. Also, check out current construction as well as planned development for the area, to make sure your property won't be adding to an over-abundance in storage units or self-serve car washes, contributing to an oversupply in the area.

Just as a business plan gives you an idea of how you are building your business, so can a feasibility study give you answers about a property's past financial and structural history. To give you a good view of the future growth potential for your specific location, get an analysis from responsible real estate agents located near your property. This is especially important if you've identified an under-supplied property type. Verifying your numbers is a must before investing any money, especially if the property is specific or has limited potential for renters (such as a laundry mat or bowling alley). A further discussion later in this book will give you more insight into what a feasibility study is, and how it can help you determine a property's value in relation to your intentions.

Identifying a property in an area that matches all of your

preferences can be challenging, particularly if you are fond of a well-developed and prosperous community - seldom do people or owners sell these profitable parcels. Yet, they do exist and they are available.

Don't get discouraged, and don't shut the door on a deal which may have potential but look bad initially. Although a negative factor may come up when you view a possible opportunity, a neglected property can also be a diamond in the rough.

Putting your time in to get the answers should be your golden rule, and it will serve you well.

2. Supply and demand (oversaturated and undersaturated areas) play a key role in determining the probable revenue of a potential CRE.

Market cycles also play a major role in the potential of your possible CRE purchase. The unemployment rate, the health of the economy, and the gross domestic product (GDP) all play an intricate role in general market health, and to understand the importance of each in the overall picture will benefit you tremendously.

The GDP is the total monetary or market value of all the finished goods and services produced within a country's borders in a specific time period. As a broad measure of overall domestic production, it functions as a comprehensive scorecard of a given country's economic health.[2]

Understanding the various cycles a market can transition through will give you an inside view for determining a high market, a low market, present opportunity advantage, and many other informed investment strategies.

Though we've already touched on the importance of several tools which will give you a good picture of what your property's market value and potential may be, a bit of in-depth investigation into these various advantages are of use when conducting your analysis.

Financial Review: This is a task a CPA conducts, carefully going over a company's financial records to determine if the financial records are correct. Basic accounting principles are used and these reviews are generally conducted every quarter (along with the provision of tax documents if necessary).

Tax Returns: Companies must pay taxes, and these taxes show a lot about the stability (or instability) of its finances. A financial statement of a company can show the same figures, giving you details which will help you determine the company's financial well-being.

Profit and Loss Statements (from previous owners): A Profit and Loss Statement, or P&L, reveals just that; the profits and losses of a company for a specific period of time. Total revenues are compared to total costs, etc., giving you additional information about the property's bottom line.

Property Inspections: By reviewing a property's inspections, you will be able to get an outside view of the property, such as how the utilities are commissioned, as well as insurance coverages and any particular riders which may be needed (think flood insurance or earthquake, etc.).

Survey Studies of Municipalities: Survey studies are also found in the public records and can give you an idea of what has happened in the past and what may be proposed for the future. For starters, you can find information on sewer repairs, waterline replacements, cable survey bids, and infrastructure improvements. With this info, you can begin your examination of future proposals and plans for the area you are considering investing in. There are a number of things you can find out which may help or hinder a property's attractiveness. Again, look under all stones for gems of information which can make your decision more informed.

Other Unique Research: With the internet's vast wealth of available information and public records being so easily viewed, not taking advantage of these resources is like leaving money on the table. Don't let it be yours! City, county, and state property records are most often considered public notices and must be recorded and filed. If there have been foreclosures, liens, or any other type of special notice on a property, you can find it in public records. Check out how your region publicizes these notices, and do some digging. Your local real estate board will be able to give you government websites to make the search a bit easier.

3. Be an expert on the area and its history, as well as its future projects.

If you are looking to buy land and develop on it, you will have a bit more investigating to do. Do not assume the clerk at the front desk knows all the municipal projects which are scheduled for the coming year.

Just like building on land, if you are planning to expand or renovate a property after purchasing it, make sure the zoning allows for your intended plans. If it doesn't, learn what may be entailed and how likely it will be you can get the zoning changes you'll need. Also, determine what permits may be needed and the involvement needed to complete the process for your project.

Building and/or renovating can be incredibly profitable, especially if your money may be coming in slowly and over a longer period of time, giving you extra time to accumulate cash. This strategy, however, will take extra research and dedication to completely analyze all aspects of the project, including whether the area can support the addition (market saturation) of your project to the area.

Also, talk to investors who have done what you want to

do. Your Chamber of Commerce can give you lists of businesses that have done major renovations, and often have conferences or meetings of businesses which have common ideas. Check out their website and make contact with someone who can keep an eye open for similar relationships you can initiate. They are specifically set up to help communities become better business partners, so use their available resources.

Real estate groups can also be of great value. By becoming a member of these organizations, you will not only develop contacts for your network, but you will often get details about properties and developments before public announcements.

Keeping extensive notes while you are compiling your checklist and contact list will make the next property analysis much easier, while also keeping you organized about what items need to be addressed during the current process.

4. If you are using creative or unique strategies in your investment purchase, such as building new or adding structure, do extra research and collect all needed information.

If your path is heading towards investing in passive forms of CRE, including real estate investment trusts (REIT's), crowdfunding, private funds, or partnerships, be just as dedicated to finding out all the information you can on the investors, company, assets, funding managers, or any other person who may be handling the investment process. Each person has their own way of doing things, and what may seem prudent and 'assumed intelligence' for one person or entity, may not be for you.

If you find yourself in this circumstance, you will want to:

- Speak with other people who have invested with the same type of group, and build a history with the group you are thinking of joining. Search for information on the contacts you will be doing business with (yes, this includes social media).
- Analyze past transactions and chart the successes and failures, as well as dollar amounts and property values pre/post transactions. Understanding actual returns on closed investments will give you a good idea of how each type of group and investment type performed.
- Get referrals from others who have worked with the specific groups you are thinking of joining.
- Find out what their process is like, how they choose investments, and what determines their investment amount.

5. Passive investments need to be investigated and analyzed, even though you may feel awkward or intrusive asking questions. It's your money, so invest with honest, experienced, and successful contacts who aren't afraid to prove the value of the investment to you.

Even with all the t's crossed and all the i's dotted, uncertainty in investments is always present. Unknown factors can always play a surprise role in the "best-laid plans".

Having a contingency fund (money for short term needs during the acquisition of your property and 1st-year improvements) or capital reserve (longer-term funds for upgrades, renovations, or improvements) will help to alleviate this uncertainty and will always serve you well. Having one should be a part of every transaction you plan on pursuing.

Reserve a line in your business investment spreadsheet to

include additional funds you can set aside to use in your initial acquisition should you need money for unexpected expenses, changes in financial loans or interest rates, or any number of other things which may come up which you hadn't planned on or foreseen. Often, a delay in funding for your property or a broken water line immediately after purchase can create devastating setbacks, especially if it is in the early building of your CRE investment strategy.

Reserve funds can help you through a negative cash flow period or help you cover debt services until the property is stabilized or rentable. Most often, plan on 5% to 15% of the purchase price, but any number of property specifics can affect the bottom line, so be fair to your projects and yourself when determining the amount you might need.

NOTE: If you set up a contingency fund while you are in the process of taking over a CRE investment, consider adding some additional funds to this account for your property as it ages, so you can budget for its maintenance. While we'd all like to think our properties can produce any needed funding as it ages, taking from Peter to pay Paul isn't a wise business plan. Having 3% to 5% of gross rents in a fund for emergencies or unexpected expenses, above your cash flow, will serve you well and look great on your financial statement.

6. Set aside a contingency fund to cover extra or unforeseen expenses as you build your CRE investments.

As you build your CRE portfolio, make sure to support it with a well-funded reserve to contend with the unexpected occurrences. I know, at this point it just seems all you'll be doing is saving and not having any cash flow for the management of your properties. After doing all your research, purchase, and property development, the last thing you want to happen is for it all to be taken away because you couldn't afford the replacement of the electrical wiring, or couldn't afford the repairs after a sprinkler break on the 5th floor of your new high rise.

Keep your figures in-line and make sure you have the margins to accommodate the unexpected.

Another factor which can play into this game plan is this: If you come across an investment opportunity which looks like a great deal but has a timeframe on it, this fund can also support those instances too. Remember, don't get emotional, however, because if it seems too good to be true …

Don't take your fund down to $0. Aim for the 5% to 15% above-value figure, and you'll have a good outlook for your financial strategy and CRE future.

EXTERNAL FACTORS OF PROPERTY PURCHASES AND HOW THEY AFFECT YOUR DECISIONS

You've seen how underlying facts about a property's background can change the prospect of a great investment to a poor one. External factors affecting your property can take the shine off an otherwise perfect investment.

The various types of CRE are increasing, and so too is the field of investors and their interests, as well as the financial benefits of current economies and potential growth as markets overcome their volatility.

Because the anxiety of investing in higher priced CRE can come easily at just about any time during your research process, attaining a high level of confidence about making wise and thorough decisions comes with knowing all the options, analyzing as many facts as you can gather, and determining predictable and well-supported outcomes.

To do this, you need to know the market in which your prospective property lies, and get answers to any questions about possible options which may affect your investment. As you can imagine, many areas play a role in determining external factors, and they include:

- Yield of the investment (earning potential)
- Interest rates
- Lease terms and options
- Population growth and demographics
- Infrastructure around the property
- Economic outlook and prospect of location
- Supply and demand

We'll examine each of these external factors.

INVESTMENT YIELD

This is probably one of the most important determinations in your external analysis, though as you already know, a combination of all the facts is what gives you the best analytical determination.

The investment yield measures the real value of a CRE property and gives you a reliable measurement of its income *potential*. This is a key factor when weighing a good decision from a poor one, and is a basis for obtaining financial backing and partnership possibilities. It is a small view into the future of your property's possibilities.

A CRE property yield is calculated as a percentage and is based on:

- Market value to property cost
- Annual income of the property
- Operating costs of the property*

*This figure can either include the operating costs of the prop-

erty or the gross yield. Either calculation is good - make sure you know which one you are working with.

Calculations for the gross percentage yield looks like this:

$$\text{Gross Yield} = [(\text{monthly rental} \times 12) \text{ weeks} / \text{property value}] \times 100 = \% \text{ Gross Yield}$$

Sample:
Gross Yield = [($4,500 X 12) / $540,000] X 100 = 10% Gross Yield
Total cost of property purchase: $500,000
Annual rent income of 10 units: $4,500 each per month

The yield is, of course, driven by demand, making this figure dependent on the property value increasing over time as well as having 0% vacancy.

Along with the gross and net yield, a target yield gives investors a goal to use for investment estimates, making the inexperienced investor a bit more optimistic than a well-seasoned CRE property owner. Prepare for the lows, but aim for the highs.

INTEREST RATES

If you have experience in residential real estate, you may see how its market influences the CRE market here.

Inflation plays a part in determining interest rates since they have a direct influence on the rates at which financial institutions will fund loans. Many other factors play into these rates, but bottom line, your loan rate will be determined by the institution you decide to do business with, who determines the rates on market values, and the Federal Reserve Bank rates (in the United States).

When interest rates rise, money costs rise also, and when

consumers aren't spending money (i.e. purchases funded on credit), economies slow. In order to revitalize consumer spending, interest rates drop, which in turn, increases lending as well as interest rates. So, as you can see, it makes sense to obtain loans when the market is down, in order to attain lower rates.

This is how the stock market works, and it's how real estate funding works. When demand is high, rates are up. When demand is low, rates are down. Would you rather fund your loan on a 4.55% interest rate over 20 years or at 8.2% for 20 years? That's definitely a no-brainer.

There are many reasons why it can be hard to find good investments during slow economic times. Consider this:

Markets are constantly being flooded with great investment properties.

Consumer spending does affect the prices and numbers of CRE properties, but consider that during slow economic times, more properties may come on the market as businesses default on their leases and move out. There may be lots of opportunities, but due to poor economic prospects, finding a stable tenant may be harder. Many opportunists love to try their hand at CRE investing when they see "a good deal" come up, but few take the time to learn the needed research methods and develop a strategy that will ensure success.

It is here where you will have the advantage and be more attractive to lending institutions when you do find a good deal. By knowing the anticipated questions and having all the answers, you will be an ideal prospect for their lending departments.

Not only knowing how interest rates fluctuate with the ebbs and flows of the economy, but being able to predict interest rate trends will give you an added edge also. Stay in touch with the economy, watch the markers (determining factors which influence interest rates), and check out the past fluctuations and interest rate trends. Chances are, with just a few references and updates, you'll get a sense of when interest rates will fall or rise, and can judge your potential investments accordingly.

LEASE TERMS AND OPTIONS

When you choose a lease term (the length of a lease in months or years), you are determining an important part of your CRE investment - it is the recovery time from initial funding to payoff.

As an investor, you need to determine if the length of the loan will be long enough for the recovery of your initial investment amount, and some profit if possible. In other words, will the leases that tenants are signing pay off the initial investment you have made?

When the lease is expired, neither the tenant nor the landlord is obliged to renew the lease. If it is not renewed, by losing this tenant, your business may lose a large portion of income by the time you find a new one that is reputable and stable.

Make sure that when you compose the lease, you include a renewal clause, so even when the lease ends, if desired, the lease can continue with both parties knowing what that would look like. If your tenants are new or have little history of a credible track record, sign a short-term lease, from 1 to 2 years, then propose an option for a renewal of the lease. This gives you time to evaluate the tenant while still keeping the door open for a longer lease relationship.

According to the *Commercial Tenancy (CT) Act*, tenants have the right to request a tenancy period extension for up to 5 years. It is up to the investor to continue with regard to extending the lease or not. Considerations for an extension are:

- The CPI index can determine rental increases - check specifics in your area.
- Lease terms can be as long as you'd like to carry them, even as long as 10 years, with renewal options included.
- Depending on your tenants' business type, the Department of Lands or a similar agency for other areas, may need to give approval for the lease, which can influence the value of tenancy. These types of businesses include medical centers, chemical treatment facilities, child care centers, and more.
- Certain lease options can also determine lease agreements, such as including payment for taxes, insurance, and utilities.
- Changes to any hard structure, including wall partitions or permanent desks, can also be stated in the lease and dealt with accordingly.

With well-established businesses or tenants, negotiate for longer lease terms of 3-5 years or more, and include options for continued terms if warranted. The thought here is, it's better to have a successful and respectable tenant for a longer period of time at a fixed term than to have higher turn-over with the potential of vacancy. Vacancy is your worst nightmare.

COMMERCIAL REAL ESTATE TYPES CAN AFFECT THE TERMS

Due to the many choices in CREs, how the property will be used, and the depreciation factor for the building structure or equipment can play a great part in this choice.

Multi-stream income properties or mixed-use dwellings affect the deciding factor, as we have discussed previously. Let's take a closer look at some of those options.

Retail buildings: There are two ways to invest in retail buildings. One is to purchase 'as is' for tenants who need specific facilities to be supplied and who are already attracted to it, such as a laundromat or car wash. Others can be leased as a 'can build to suit' property, meaning the property can be customized for a particular business. Expenses for these types can be negotiated between the renting business and the landlord.

Industrial: Most often, these buildings are already suited for the tenants' needs. Generally, the tenant's business strength will dictate the value of the property. These businesses may only be suitable for certain types of businesses, so longer terms are desirable. Lease terms for these kinds of properties can be 5-10 or more years at a time.

Apartment Buildings: Consider the location of the building. Is it in an area which tenants will want to live? If the apartments are large, 2 to 4 bedrooms, most tenants will have larger families. Are there schools and parks nearby, or are they close to highways or freeways which may be attractive to commuters? Can the rental rates support the cost of a popular or expensive area?

Offices: Certain amenities need to be in place for an office to be offered for lease, such as computer cabling, phone support, onsite generators, and sophisticated interior finishing. Lease terms tend to be short-term, to keep pace with property values, as these businesses demand a high level of initial investment before occupancy. These types of businesses have low levels of "wear and tear", so it is easier to attract new tenants, or negotiate new terms with existing tenants when their lease is up.

POPULATION GROWTH AND ACCOMMODATION

Most often, a community's growth runs in conjunction with CRE in a predictable manner. As a community grows, it develops shopping centers, and small compatible businesses such as gas stations and grocery markets. As the population grows, so does its CRE, with apartment buildings and multifamily properties, specialty shops, restaurants, and government buildings being built. Then, as business demand increases, office space develops and industrial support services begin to emerge.

Many new businesses contribute to population growth, and as people move into the communities, new businesses increase exponentially. If a city is well-established, opportunity for new growth slows, and CRE becomes more specific and specialized. This can increase investment revenue, as each community and city becomes individualized, modernized, and unique.

INFRASTRUCTURE

Roads, airports, and railways play a huge part in CRE, with hopefully, government officials designing a city's infrastructure with care and consideration. Even the most well-laid plans can be side-tracked and can fall victim to poverty, poor tax revenue, and zoning mistakes.

Your diligence is necessary to separate the prosperous neighborhoods and communities from the ones with a bleak future. Discovering upcoming projects and developments for infrastructure can breathe new life into the slowest of community economies, and it can prove to be a very keen investment if purchased at opportune times.

Let's discuss a scenario which may on the surface, sound unattractive, but in reality, is a diamond in the rough.

As you are sifting through the many business renovation permits which have been applied for, and doing research on communities nearby, you discover that a new bypass freeway entrance is going to be constructed in a fairly run-down, low-income, and basically, deserted area.

Because this bypass freeway will directly link to the interstate which diverges to the new airport, you begin to think industrial warehousing near this bypass freeway entrance would be ideal for transportation and shipping companies, as it would take advantage of the new roads, and currently cheap land. You locate some properties for sale which are undervalued, and voila, you make some investments. These are investments that will have high revenue potential when the bypass freeway entrance is completed.

Not only did you get incredible financial backing for the lower-income rated area at a reduced interest rate, but you were able to get additional funding for improving the existing structures with a federal funding grant. Along the way, you were also able to secure locations for two fast-food franchises. Not bad for picking up on a bypass freeway project announcement!

Pay attention to the details about infrastructure projects when searching for CRE options. Good investment properties can come to you from places you never thought possible.

ECONOMIC OUTLOOK AND PROSPECT OF LOCATION

You've no doubt realized how important the location of your property is. If it's located in a derelict area, chances are, you'll also be getting low-rent tenants. Or if the building is in a high-income neighborhood, the cost, in turn, will likely also be high.

But these aren't the only reasons location is important when determining a property's relevance. You should also consider:

- The visibility of the property location.
- Public transport accessibility.
- Tenant ease of accessibility.
- Surrounding businesses which support or decrease surrounding property value.
- Zoning and population numbers.
- Position in relation to the suburbs and outlying regions.
- Similar commercial properties which are available or unavailable in the area.

Make sure you are aware of the zoning laws which govern your prospective property as well as any proposals which may be up for changing those laws. City and county councils and meeting agendas can also give you an idea of what may be proposed for change.

If you examine the demographic changes over the past 2, 5, and 10 years, you will be able to also determine how the community is growing. If new families are moving in, if businesses are saturating the areas, if residential areas are moving towards the commercial developments, or there are other key changes which will affect your potential investment, then you need to consider if these will work for your investment opportunities or against them. Consider the following:

- How many businesses are struggling?

- How many have just opened their doors for business?
- Is there a large enough customer base to support all the businesses?

Make sure all of your considerations involve past, current, and possible future patterns. All of these will have bearing on the potential growth pattern for your business and the possibility of an upturn or a downturn as the demographics of the community change.

SUPPLY AND DEMAND FOR COMMERCIAL PROPERTY

You've already begun to train your eye to notice details and determine the importance of them.

Take this knowledge one step farther. Let's think about some proposed scenarios.

- If you are looking into purchasing a strip mall of 6 units and are hoping to support a community within one mile of a college campus, what types of businesses do you think will be attracted to your property? A computer and print shop? A pizza pub? A second-hand clothing store?
- A friend has mentioned his brother-in-law is selling the building his boat business has occupied, and is moving his business closer to the beach. You already know several things before you even set eyes on the building or see the surrounding area. You know the business probably isn't doing so well, or he wouldn't be moving closer to a larger body of water. If you heard about it from your friend, it probably means the offer hasn't been made public yet and chances are, a real estate agent

hasn't been appointed. Perhaps the price hasn't even been determined yet, but there will be a bottom-line which the brother-in-law must hit in order to facilitate his move. Do you anticipate this deal as an opportunity worth pursuing or do you stay as far away as possible?
- You have an aunt who has decided to move into a senior citizen community and she wants to sell her huge home. She's lived alone for 13 years. The house is approximately 5,000 square feet, two levels, with a mother-in-law apartment which hasn't been rented out since you were young. The home is on a busy street corner, on a ¾ acre lot adjacent to a vacant lot which has never been developed. It used to have a really great pond that you would catch frogs in. Would you consider purchasing the home and renting out the house and apartment after renovations? Would you check out zoning and permit laws to see if you could demolish the present home and build a commercial property? Would you buy the adjoining lot which has a potential water source that could affect building permits?

Did you notice how each scenario about a potential investment property had aspects that you thought were good, and some that were not so good? The fewer the details, the more questions you had. The more details you had, the more interested (or uninterested!) you became. With each property, you will have to consider what is the best option for you in your quest for financial freedom!

Now you're beginning to think like a CRE investor, looking at all the angles and options when considering investing in a piece of property. Some you won't give a second look at, others you may think have the potential for improvements, and still others you may really want to investigate to see if the figures 'work'.

CHAPTER SUMMARY

- Make sure your analysis includes all aspects and details about the property related to its location. Can the area support the property, especially if you are renovating to suit a tenant?
- Will zoning plans have any effect on your goals?
- Can the market support property growth (and ultimately, rental increases)?

In the next chapter, you will learn about what makes a property attractive for investment.

CHAPTER FOUR: STEP ONE, PART TWO - STUDY THE PROPERTY

❉❉❉

Many would say that 'knowing the property' is a given. You should, by all means, know as many details as possible when considering an investment property. But how well do you really know the property? Consider the following questions:

- Do you feel you can improve the building, thereby increasing the rent?
- Can you negotiate a lower cost because the property is close to a railroad?
- Is the area set for a new park to be installed, thereby increasing the value of it down the road?

Yes, all of these things play a part in establishing the value of a property, but there are many other details to consider. Let's review some important aspects to understand before you decide on your commercial real estate (CRE) property.

BECOME AN EXPERT ON THE AREA YOU ARE CONSIDERING

Which do you think is the hardest to change, the condition of a building, or the location it is in? Of course, improving a building can be done, but improving an area takes more than renovation and supplies. An area which has a strong economy and is a desirable, attractive, well served community will hold its value much longer. It will also be appealing to tenants sooner and longer than one you are hoping will improve with time. If you are counting on the property to be desirable to tenants, the area must be to their liking as well.

This desirability, however, doesn't just rely on good foot traffic or a busy shopping mall. You need to do some in-depth research into the location in order to consider your evaluation a well-thought-out one.

How are employment numbers trending? Consider the prospects for a math tutoring center next door to a large adult-only community development. Do you think this is a compatible business considering the needs of the community? Do you think a pharmacy or health food store might do better with this demographic?

Is the area dependent on employment at a major business, such as a manufacturing plant or call center? If so, does this business have a solid future at this location, or could they be moving their company to another region?

Conversely, is a large company moving in, and if so, how will this impact your property and its attractiveness to tenants?

Check out current and recent listings to see what has sold and what hasn't in the last 6 months. Can you determine why some properties didn't sell?

Consult the listing sheet for more history about the neighborhood, schools, businesses, communities, and zoning. Ask businesses which are close by for general impressions of the area. Drive by the property at different times of the day to determine traffic, security issues, and access. Finding out as much about the property as you can before you buy it will reduce any surprises after your purchase.

KNOW THE PROPERTY'S HISTORY, CURRENT CONDITION, AND FORESEEABLE REPAIRS

Now that you know the area and are confident in its value with regard to your specific property, dig into the details of the property itself. Though you trust the agent and the seller or financial institutions' due diligence, do your own homework on its history. You'll be surprised by the details you'll uncover. They may become very important to you and your evaluation of the property.

Check out the outside of the building without anyone else's opinions or rhetoric to influence you. Ask yourself:

- Are there any improvements which will need to be made, such as repairing the exterior or addressing water leaking from underneath a doorway?
- Is the roof in good shape? Are the windows sound, or are there gaps or broken panes which will need attention?

Check out utility lines, making sure they are free from tree branches or possible falling debris. Look around at the ground for evidence of contamination, spills, flooding or debris.

Ask questions and make sure you can get access to the entire property. You can check out the foundation for cracks, check the HVAC system's efficiency, and inspect the electrical panel and wiring. You'll also want to determine if there is any asbestos, mold, or lead paint on the premises, if the building is older and has been updated or renovated. You may need to hire a qualified inspector to get you reliable information on these topics.

Now that you have all the numbers in place, it's time to see how your property candidate fares from its inception to the current condition.

If you are investing your time into analyzing a development which has been constructed in the last 10 to 20 years, you may be able to find a feasibility study which has been conducted on the project. It would give you a 'blueprint' of sorts, about how the development was planned and executed, as well as the teams' financial goals and investments at the time. Then you can evaluate if the property has lived up to the aspirations the builders had. Has it held it's value? Has it been well maintained? If you are looking to assume a property which has gone bankrupt or is struggling with under-par construction, you may have less luck finding reports about the business, and there may be more risk to the investment.

If you are looking to become an investor in a newly constructed development, your team should have in place or be devising a feasibility study to determine a successful path for construction and development of the project. It may be compiled on a per lot or per unit basis, or it could be on the entire project.

A thorough and conclusive study will include all of the following:

- Pre-property development assessment
- Civil site and public infrastructure improvements
- Land use and environmental permitting
- Code review and compliance
- Survey(s), boundary, title research, etc.

- Structural engineering
- Site planning
- Traffic plans, neighborhood impacts, school prospects
- Water and sewage
- Architectural soundness
- Concept testing
- Geotechnical investigation
- Development program
- Confidence for project completion
- Community impact
- Finance for the development
- Secured or prospects for funding for all phases

These are only a few of the details you would want to inspect before investing in a new development project. A new development investment can give you incredible revenue after completion, but the road to 'completion' can be arduous, tedious and fraught with ups and downs. Make sure you have all the facts you need and complete your analysis under the mentorship of a knowledgeable finance and legal team. Many people have lost millions of dollars in developments which didn't have all the needed components and plans in place. Don't let this happen to you.

KNOW WHO YOU ARE BUYING FROM

If the seller is a financial institution, it will be harder to find out unit-details on the property, but you still may be able to determine some background with public property and business records. You would also be able to check into any offers which may have been made on the property, either during this sale, or any previous times it may have been on the market.

If you can talk to the seller, this is ideal. Having a good working relationship with the seller can build confidence for this sale as well as laying a foundation for a working relationship in the future. If you are lucky, the property will be represented by a good CRE agent who is able to provide all the information you need about it. No one is obliged to tell you, but if you can find out, it is always good to know why they are selling. Do they have to sell, or is it by choice? Did their business fail at this location? Are they expanding to a larger property due to growth in their industry? Did they not like the property anymore?

If the owners have to sell due to financial hardship, you may be able to get a price reduction if you can deliver a quick close or a cash deal.

At this point, it would be a good idea to have a 'seller credibility packet' assembled which you can give to any seller. Keep this document updated and current. It should contain:

- Your contact information.
- A description of your business.
- A list of your core business services.

You can put these items in a spreadsheet and personalize them for each buyer you have contact with. It will give them your information all in one place, as well as show your professional integrity and the intent of your purchase. *It shows that you are serious about your investment.*

This can be done in a brief summary sheet, or you can expand it to share details of your interests, goals and preferences. You may even have a copy of your business plan to show them. Whether you follow through with a purchase or not, sharing this information may also open some avenues for business networking that you wouldn't have otherwise pursued.

Next, check how many days the property has been on the market, and see if you can find out who has looked at the property already.

Has the seller had any offers, and if so, are you going up against another bid?

Because commercial deals tend to move slower than residential sales, you will have some time to do your homework, while still being able to obtain a desirable property to invest in.

HOW DO YOU FEEL ABOUT WHAT YOU KNOW?

Do you think you are ready to make the purchase? Consider this:

- If you are content with the knowledge you have gathered, the people you have spoken with, and the offer on the financial side ...
- If you feel you have done your calculations correctly, run the expenses, including renovations, upkeep, contingency, and revenue figures, and it all looks sound ...
- If you feel you know: the property inside and out; the area like you lived there for years; and the details of the sale and financing, and if it looks to be a profitable venture …

If you answered, "Yes" to all of these considerations, then you are likely ready to make the purchase of your CRE.

BE CONFIDENT ABOUT THE SPECIFICS

Here are the next steps you need to know before signing on the dotted line.

Bring in your team to stand beside you and check the specifics: This is why you brought them on. They will make sure the figures are correct, the wording is sound, and all conditions are abided by. They are working for you. If you don't understand something, ask them. Never feel like you can't ask questions. Now is the time to make sure everything is to your liking and needs, and that it is geared toward achieving your financial goals and strategy.

Read the contract: Take the time to read through the contract and make sure you understand everything which has been stated in it. Make sure every detail you understood would be included is actually in the contract because once it is signed, changing or adding any details is next to impossible.

Itemize what is included and what has to be done before the property transfers ownership. For example, is there furniture or appliances which are to be left in the building? Does flooring need to be removed or brickwork need to be redone? If so, make sure it's stated in the contract.

Make sure the conditions are outlined the way you intended, with details of who will be responsible for anything that needs to be done and when it will be completed by. Also have a clause addressing what happens if these conditions aren't met.

If the contract isn't clear, have it rewritten. This is *your* purchase and your money. You are the one responsible for making sure it suits your needs.

THE CRE INVESTMENT SHOULD FIT YOUR NEEDS, NOT THE OTHER WAY AROUND

Just as each investment has its own unique qualities, so do commercial properties. As an investor, you've learned some new angles from which to view these differences. Compared to other real estate transactions you may have been associated with in the past, a CRE acquisition may bring new and exciting challenges.

Because the investment dollars are higher in CRE, your awareness of all aspects of the CRE investment cycle also has to be higher. Let's recap the specifics:

- *First*: Understand the process of investing in CRE.
- *Second:* Learn the ways that investing in CRE can benefit you in your goal of achieving financial freedom.
- *Third*: Commit to memory the calculations and tools you will need in order to separate the good deals from the not-so-good ones.
- *Fourth*: Build a team of experts to help you make important decisions along the way, from accountants and legal support, to real estate brokers and financial lenders.
- *Fifth*: Commit to researching and analyzing not only the property, but the area, including its history, and what future prospects a property may have as a result of development.
- *Sixth*: Set responsible parameters for attaining CRE based on your financial ability to fund the investment, as well as what type of property you should focus on.
- *Seventh*: Find the best way to handle property management and how much involvement might be required for each property.

- *Eighth*: Build your capital so you can invest in more CRE. This will build toward your goal of financial freedom.

At this point in time, you may be feeling a bit overwhelmed. If you are, back up to where you feel you may have started to let your attention wander, or where you started to read with glazed-over, tired eyes, and re-read as much of the chapter as you need to. This isn't a doctorate degree in investments, but it is complicated and detailed information. You should not feel like you have to absorb all the information at once, or even the first time you read it.

What you have in your hands is the result of years and years of devising, compiling, trial and error, and steadfast determination in order to achieve a sound and true system for investing in real estate. For you to read this in a few nights and then go out and purchase an 8-plex condominium project with great success is asking for a few miracles, with a bit of magic sprinkled on top!

I'm not saying it isn't possible to speed-read this book, dive into your first investment making no mistakes, and make more money than you dreamed possible. I'm just saying, most people will have to work harder than that! I want you to know this is a lot of information, and these subjects require you to dive deeply into a lot of new facts and strategies. There is a lot to remember, and there is no harm in taking your time to learn everything you can, as well as you can, before you risk your money on a CRE investment.

Mastering these strategies is so doable! Give yourself the time and patience needed in order for you to soak it all in. Then you will engage in CRE deals with knowledge, confidence, and conviction.

Some other things you may want to consider to ensure the investment is the right fit for you are:

- *Know your tools and calculations and use the same ones for every deal*: If your investment is for 5 units, or 500, the analysis, calculations, research, and processes are the same. Once you have the formulas for purchasing mastered, you just have to apply the same steps to each endeavor.
- *Make life easy on yourself:* By having many units under one roof, you are:
- Saving yourself time by managing units at one location instead of many.
- Saving money because the costs of one loan are much less than having 5 or more separate loans.
- Making more revenue since although each units' revenue may be less individually, adding them together will more often than not, be far more lucrative than returns on a single larger investment.
- Reducing risk of cash-flow issues due to vacancy risk because having other rental incomes will cover the loss of income from a vacant unit.
- Increasing cash flow because since you have more income sources, your cash flow figures are higher.

Yes, the initial investment is more on larger properties. It costs less to buy one residence as opposed to a six-unit apartment complex for instance, but attaining financial loans is easier and less risky, and personal losses can often be avoided on these larger investment properties.

CHAPTER SUMMARY

- Look for opportunities in disadvantaged properties, as well as those with obvious revenue

potential. Projects planned for the future, such as a new road, can change a property's outlook considerably.
- Look at the property yourself - get to know it literally, inside and out.
- Rely on your team to support you with their knowledge and expertise.

In the next chapter, you will learn how to set up your business so that you can properly support your investment in CRE properties.

CHAPTER FIVE: STEP TWO - THE MEANS, THE SUPPORT, AND THE STRUCTURE OF YOUR INVESTMENT

❊❊❊

THERE ARE MANY ASPECTS TO CONSIDER WHEN ACQUIRING A good financial vehicle for your CRE investment. It doesn't only involve the interest rate, your credibility, and the financial institution's willingness to lend you money, though these factors are part of the process. Many details need to be discussed, determined, assessed and agreed to before you take ownership and receive the keys.

To begin the process, you need to show due diligence (as if you haven't heard that before!). Having all your documents and necessary paperwork compiled and organized will facilitate the process. It will not only show the loan officer you are a professional and that you want to make their decision as easy as possible, but preparing it also gives you insight into more options and opportunities for purchasing the perfect property investment.

Having a good sense of your credit rating is the best place to start. If you don't have your finances in order, or you don't yet have your business set up, get a current credit report and review it first. Call the credit bureaus individually or ask your accountant or financial advisor if they can help you get them. Quite often, a credit card or banking institution will give you this information, or at least they will give you contact information for the credit bureaus. Knowing where you stand in the beginning gives you the obvious place to start.

If you haven't set up your business, do it now. You'll need to protect your personal assets, namely your home, car(s), and any other property and savings or accounts (pension, etc.) which is set up in your or your spouses' name. If it has value, it is considered an asset and could be taken away if your business fails.

Most often, businesses who are looking to protect their personal assets choose an limited liability company (LLC), but there may be some details which you won't want to adhere to, so read about each option (sole-proprietorship, partnership, LLC, etc.) and choose the right business structure for you.

The reasons I lean towards LLC's are discussed below.

PROTECTION FROM LIABILITY CLAIMS AND EXPOSURE TO RISK

Building a LLC is one of the first, and most preferred, steps a business owner can take, especially if you are involved in CRE. Holding title to one or more CRE investments is a profitable way to make money, but it can expose you to risk and expensive claims if you expose yourself and your assets to liability.

Don't let this concept trip you up or put fear into you. It's just a step which has to be taken in order to keep you and your family safe and protected.

There are also tax benefits which can be taken advantage of, making your ownership of a CRE with the business protection of an LLC very desirable and advantageous in most business situations.

An LLC holding vehicle is very popular for businesses, but many compare the formalities of such a venture troublesome, particularly when affordable liability insurance is available. Do you believe this insurance will cover the personal liability risk of one of your tenants or property partners? Let's do a comparison and you can be the judge.

A *typical liability policy* has limitations and exceptions, not to mention the occasional "carve-out" and disclaimers. Purchasing liability insurance is a risk; you're betting the company you won't have a claim, but what happens when that bet fails you and it means you're losing your personal home and assets?

Do you think the odds of never having a disgruntled tenant or liability issue in the lifetime of your investment are slim to none?

Or, would you rather fall back on the assurances of a blanket protection which an LLC gives you, less a few extra dollars and a couple of hours?

Is the coverage 'guarantee' of an insurance policy riddled with vague promises worth the few extra dollars in your pocket?

It's a given that the additional money you will save initially if you purchase the insurance policy will never cover the losses incurred by a lawsuit.

Are you convinced yet?

Let's look at the other side of setting up your CRE business as an LLC.

Picture an ideal apartment complex. In this complex, you have a particularly clumsy tenant. This tenant falls down the stairs to his apartment and breaks his leg. He decides to sue you for damages and medical bills.

If you own the building individually, you will be named in the lawsuit and you'd have to defend your personal assets from the plaintiff's claims. If, however, your business, which is set up as an LLC, is the owner of the property, your company's assets are the only ones exposed to the lawsuit, which protects your own personal assets. True, you don't want to lose any property to claims of liability, but if it comes down to losing your investment property over losing your home, it is an obvious choice. You keep your family safe and sound in the home and give up your CRE. An LLC allows you to do that.

Now you can build up your investments easily and quickly, because you have the tools and knowledge. No one wants to face hardships, but if the worst happens, you won't be destitute or homeless. If only for this reason alone, it is one very strong and convincing reason to form your business as an LLC.

There are other instances which benefit an owner operating under an LLC.

You benefit from pass-through taxation. The Internal Revenue Service (IRS) has a set of default tax classification rules, and as a real estate holding company set up as an LLC, you are able to enjoy the same classification as an individual or sole-proprietorship, who only has to pay taxes on income and capital gains as an individual and not as a corporation.

Due to the fact that there is no separate LLC tax classification, the owner can avoid double taxation on rental income (from the property) and the appreciation of the property when selling it. If you are a single owner, the LLC enables you to deduct mortgage interest just like a sole proprietor can (based on current IRS outlines and conditions).

Other conditions include multi-member LLC's which are, for the most part, taxed like partnerships, requiring 'informational' tax returns be filed, but they do not actually pay taxes. Rather, the benefit comes from the pass-through taxation by way of having *their members* claim their portion of the business' profits or loss on a Schedule C, K, or Form 1065, and then file it with their own individual tax return. Again, this gives all owners personal protection with limited liability.

The benefits don't end there.

- LLC's have increased flexibility over other types of businesses, such as corporations and partnerships. No meetings need to be held and recorded quarterly, and they are easily managed by its owners or third-party managers.
- LLC's often pay lower state registration and maintenance fees for shareowners and holders.
- The distribution of profits that LLC's can take advantage of is large, and governed by the LLC's operating agreement. This means that there is fluctuating cash distributions of profits, giving the owners the control required to be able to financially reward their investors or owners whenever they want to.
- If you live outside the USA, foreign ownership and investment in American real estate are possible through an LLC.
- Proactively gifting ownership is also an option in real estate holdings by LLC owners, making the transfer of ownership to family members or heirs easy. There is no need to have deeds changed with updated names. Not only is this an easier process of transfer, but it avoids recording taxes and fees, which can be substantial, as some states base the fees on a percentage of the current value of the CRE.

Because there are certain criteria which must be in place,

and certain dialogue which needs to be respected and used, it is best to have your CRE accountant and tax advisor help you set up your LLC to its best advantage, as well as getting your legal real estate expert to assist when building your business plan. Updates and requirements should always be double-checked for credibility and compliance. All in all, setting up your CRE investment business as an LLC is not only wise, but in today's business world, it's almost mandatory.

Have your business LLC set up before you begin your financial process of acquiring your first CRE property. If you have it set up in advance, you and your team will find advantages when purchasing CRE's, including being set above other applicants. This gives you clout and puts you on a higher professional business level than others.

SECURING FINANCIAL LENDERS

Some financial institutions may require securing the mortgage, which will, in turn, be used as collateral when you are purchasing a CRE. This is one reason many people choose CRE investing; so their personal assets are not at risk. However, many different factors and requirements will play into the unfolding of an investment property loan approval. Here are the basics you should be aware of and be ready for before you visit any financial institution or mortgage agency for a loan.

- If you have a particular property in mind, have it appraised professionally. Determine the CRE's market value, and have it stated in a certified official document. By having these solid numbers, a loan officer can begin the process with confidence. This figure also lessens the risk of the loan being drawn up for more money than is needed, in case the seller has inflated the price to compensate for anticipated loss or debt.

- Improve your credit score as much as possible. By having a high credit score, you are showing the lender you have the financial savvy and awareness that is required to be a successful business owner. As odd as it sounds, your personal credit score does carry weight when applying for a loan on an investment property because it tells the lender whether *you* are a reliable risk. Improve it as much as possible. If you are unsure of how to improve your score, there are many financial sites which can coach you through raising it, as can your trusted CPA or financial advisor.

- Be clear about your reasons for applying for the loan. Don't be lengthy with this statement, and don't twist the facts because you think they will sound better. They won't. Financial lending officers have a clear picture of what their institution's boundaries and rules are for lending money. Also realize that each institution's rules can be different. Be straightforward, honest, and clear in where you stand financially. Also, be aware, what may seem like a black mark on your record won't necessarily be that to a loan officer. When you are upfront with your application and your answers, it is up to the agent to determine your ability to repay the loan.

- Calculate the down payment you will need for the loan. The calculation of this amount determines the loan value and its feasibility to be issued. The high value of CRE governs many criteria for increased diligence when lending on CRE properties. Having a portion of the loan upfront shows you are capable and serious about attaining the loan and paying off the debt. This shows that you are able to generate funds to further your business. Showing that you are aware of their position will score high and give them confidence in you. Though most CRE loans require 20% or more as a down payment in order to be approved, creative financing is sometimes available to provide 100% of a property's LTV ratio to be loaned in certain instances. These loans, of course, usually have stricter criteria for approval, but if you find funding for these types of loans, you may have more options for your financial needs than you thought possible.

- The DSCR, or debt-service coverage ratio, will also influence the outcome of your application for funds. As you remember, this calculation determines the amount of revenue you anticipate the property will generate once acquired, and it is directly related to the loan amount. It is with this ratio lenders can see if you can afford to repay the loan with your monthly payments. Accepted numbers for this ratio can range from 1.1 to 1.4, with a ratio of 1.0 being unacceptable (and you will be refused the loan) to 1.4, which means the revenue is generating more than the loan debt (a very good thing!).
- The documents each lender will ask for can vary, but most often you will be asked for personal and business bank statements for at least the past 6 months, retirement accounts if there are any your business pays out or that you receive, and investment account statements. This is a list of the

essential items you will need when applying for financial assistance:
- Established date of your business
- Business and personal credit score
- Annual revenue or monthly sales figures
- Business and personal tax returns
- Personal background and character profiles
- Bank statements
- Purpose of the loan
- Business plan
- Collateral
- Any legal documents which are related to your business, such as licenses, agreements, leases for adjoining real estate, etc.
- Your social security card, driver's license, income documents, bankruptcy documents, and loan details may be requested, so have them ready and waiting also. If you are a self-employed borrower, you'll also need your business license, business financial statement, and any other bank documents which will help the lender determine your financial status.
- Organize your 'team'. We've talked about the importance of having a financial advisor, CPA, and legal representation, and they couldn't be needed more than when you are applying for financial assistance. This is the time when they go to work for you, once again, and provide you with their expertise, provide the necessary paperwork, and guide you with counsel in business transactions. A *real estate attorney* who deals with property contracts and an *accountant who is a specialist with investment property tax strategies* can give you an edge. Paying for these services is worth the extra

dollars. It will save you anxiety, lost money, and research time, as you assemble your investment business structure. Having a mortgage professional can also be a great benefit, as they have current market knowledge and are updated on revisions of any laws, permits, and zoning changes which may affect you and your finances. Best of all, they have ways to solve any issues which may come up during the process.

REAL ESTATE LOANS AND CHOOSING THE BEST ONE FOR EACH PROPERTY

Few investors have the means to purchase a property outright. If you do, a great power is in your corner, but if you don't, it's time to learn about different commercial investment loan types and how each kind can benefit a particular situation or circumstance.

There are almost as many types of commercial financing tools as there are institutions to lend you money. Well, not really, but many options exist for you to obtain just about any property you find worthy of your interest.

All financial vehicles have their own individual requirements. Some will place a great importance on the credit score while another values a high down payment. Your job is to not only learn the details of each type of loan but also determine which type will benefit you the most when financing an investment property.

As a business, you will contact a financial institution and discuss the options they offer for your needs.

A business consultant will discuss your situation and have a conversation about how they interpret your needs and the best way they can accommodate those needs. They will have you fill out an application, and depending on the type of financial loan, the required documentation will be itemized.

Once assembled, the completed application and all of your documentation will be submitted by you to the financial underwriters for approval.

After approval has been given, you will be issued the funds. You will also receive a schedule for payments throughout the length of the loan until it is paid in full.

The length of the loan, also known as the *term length*, interest rates, and loan-to-value ratios can be determining factors in figuring out which avenue will get you to the outcome you want and in the fastest way possible.

NOTE: When reviewing possible loan types for your purchase, make sure the institution you are applying with works with small business owners and is sympathetic to your endeavors. Applying 'online' or with an agency you found from a mailing can prove to be problematic and most likely, these types of institutions *will not* work with you if you fall under occupancy percentages or can't come up with a full 20% down payment. Look at who is funding your loan and make sure they are the kind of company you want to be doing business with, as you will be working with them throughout the life of your loan.

Here is a brief description of a few of the popular loan types you will come across.

Conventional Loan: These loans have terms and conditions which you will most likely be familiar with. There are financial covenants, such as LTV or DSCR requirements which you will have to consider, along with typical either fixed or floating interest rates, payment schedules, and repayment terms. Everything is quite standard and expected. The application process is usually shorter than with other loan types mentioned below, as you will be applying for your loan with only the financial institution being the supplier of your funding. If you have an established business or operating history, a project-based loan (dependent on rental revenue for loan repayment) may be appropriate but sometimes can be challenging. On the other hand, if you have a property which needs improvements or renovations, this type of loan may be ideal, as it will allow you to begin quicker, and it can be paid off when tenants are established, with a more suitable loan considered as replacement, if needed.

NOTE: These loans have covenants, and you must adhere to them throughout the term of the loan. Understanding these restrictions and requirements is mandatory when determining if this type of loan is a good choice for you.

Small Business Administration (SBA) 7(a) Loan: These loans are set up to launch a business while keeping you in control of your company. This type of loan has a portion which is backed by the government and it allows small business owners to obtain financing with less equity than is needed with a conventional loan. The bank or financial institution that you apply for your loan with is the actual lender, but the government guarantees the institution a percentage of the loan if you default on it. This type of loan can also help in an acquisition or expansion of an established business or company. Typically, there is a down payment required, 10% to 35%, and requires a cash flow analysis, which you should already have in place from your initial research analysis of the property. The term length for these loans typically runs from 10 to 25 years and they are guaranteed for anywhere from 75% to 85% of the loan. Interest rates are adjustable, based on the current prime rate. The maximum amount for a 7(a) loan is $5 million.

Small Business Administration (SBA) 504 Loan / Certified Development Company (CDC) Loan: These loans are specially designed for CRE and large equipment purchases. They can also be used to acquire land, begin a new construction endeavor, or improve an existing building. Maximum lending amounts are $20 million and can be as low as

$125,000. Down payments begin at 10%, in equity or cash, with most being between 15% and 20%. Terms are for 20 years with fixed rates for real estate property purchases.

If you are looking at SBA loan types, be sure to work with an SBA specialist who can advise you on which type of SBA loan is right for you. There is also a *Preferred Lenders Program* (PLP's), which can provide valuable knowledge and also streamline your application.

Hard Money Loan: These loans are in place for specific circumstances, and usually involve real estate in one form or another. They are loans which are secured by real property and are considered a last-ditch effort when other loans can't be attained. They also can include loans for 'flipping' a property, land loans, credit issue loans, real estate investments, and construction loans. They are short-term loans which are written at higher interest rates and have a lower LTV ratio. They are completed quickly in order to complete a pending deal or proposition, and are funded by private individuals or companies and not financial institutions. By using the property as collateral, the terms are often negotiated between the lender and the borrower, reducing the time to obtain funding considerably. Quite often, the lender is the benefactor in this transaction, as they are either compensated by the loan being paid off in a timely fashion, or they acquire the property in default, which most often is worth more than the total loan payments to date.

Commercial Bridge Loan: These are "hard money loans" specifically set up for CRE properties only. Terms and details are individual to each loan and again, the property is used as collateral against default.

Conduit Loan: Also known as CMBS loans, these tools are combined with other CRE's to form a combined marketing option for investors on the secondary market. They are known for their simple requirements and are limited to income-generating properties only. These combined CRE packages are referred to as 'tranches' and are divided into categories for investor preferences, on risk, return, and loan maturity. A good example of the offerings could be targeted to high-risk investors with loans that have longer terms and higher interest rates, or lower-risk investors whose packages would include pension funds and long-term annuities. The deviations in these loans are broad, and each can be written to its own specifications. If you are interested in this type of loan, make sure you are aware of the pros and cons of this loan structure. More often than not, the properties and companies involved in these types of loans are well versed and seasoned in creative financial campaigns, and they have the knowledge and experience to be successful in this arena. These loans are not for beginners or timid investors. In other words, *know your stuff* or you may just find yourself without a dime in your pocket.

Line of Credit Loan: Having a line of credit can save a business and its cash flow, which is usually the hardest issue to solve when opening a new business or company. It's a flexible way to attain and pay back the money but it requires a good credit history to establish credibility and get the loan. It can be a matter of what came first, the chicken or the egg, as many new entrepreneurs find cash flow the hardest problem to solve - trying to prove you are a good credit risk can be hard if you are just starting out. There is no down payment, and you only pay interest on the money you borrow, but covenants can be in place and often include net worth, interest ratio, debt ratio, and material changes. Payments can be made as quickly as the borrower sees fit, and you can use this line of credit when cash flow is low or a windfall has come in. Terms can be short or long, depending on qualifying criteria, and the loan can also be secured with collateral, although it is not always necessary. Financial institution offers vary greatly, so determine the most important criteria for your situation before committing to any one lender.

GETTING A COMMERCIAL REAL ESTATE LOAN

Now that you know the many types of loans available, you probably have a good idea of which one would be the best choice for you. Applying your own particular details to the loan process isn't hard, it's just a matter of gathering the information and putting it on the right line. Once you have familiarized yourself with the forms and the process, it will be a matter of crossing the t's and dotting the i's. Then, you are on your way and ready to really begin your Journey to Financial Freedom.

Your move begins with *getting the money*.

When a lender looks at an applicant, most often, there are five categories which they judge your creditworthiness by. These are *character, capital, collateral, capacity,* and *condition*.

CHARACTER

When a lender analyzes your 'character' they are determining your honesty, integrity, and knowledge in the business transaction they are looking to begin with you. The lender needs to feel you have the background to be successful in the business they are subsidizing, as well as the ability to follow through on your 'word' as a borrower.

You will be asked about background checks into your credit, as well as a possible criminal record check. As we've said, both your personal and business history will be checked, and any discrepancies will be discussed, so you can answer and explain any questions in person. If you have a solid and reputable history, but perhaps have a period of unemployment, you will be given the time to explain this, and if another area of your application is impressive and shows high levels of competence or creditworthiness, your period of unemployment may have less bearing on your application.

CAPITAL

Chances are, you will be asked if you have plans in place to add your own financial backing to the business. If a lender sees you putting up money to invest in your own business, chances are they will be more willing to lend you money. You will be seen as a person who is willing to financially invest in their own future, which will give them more reason to invest in your ideas also.

COLLATERAL

Because you will likely be securing your loan with the property as collateral, you won't be as invested in proving you have other 'backing' to supplement your creditworthiness. However, if there is something which may increase your chances of getting their attention and showing your ability to further improve your investment, the lender will look at your extra assets as a bonus. For example, if you were a landscaper and you have a plan to improve the surrounding areas or install a pool in the apartment complex, this will add value to the property they are helping finance.

CAPACITY (OR CASH FLOW)

It will be necessary to show the lender, without a doubt, that your business can repay the loan. Having a sufficient cash flow indicates this ability and it will need to be ample enough to cover the expenses of the loan and the upkeep, improvement, and maintenance of the property. If there are additional investors, their salaries will be investigated, as will the status of any loans you presently may have for either your personal or business purposes. Showing a history of your companies' ability to accomplish this will give you the appearance of being an ideal borrower for them to lend money to.

CONDITION

You will need to show the 'condition' or the present economic status of not only your company, but of the real estate industry in your location and how it plays a part in the economy presently and in the future. They will also ask for a *forecast of conditions* and your personal expectations for business growth or decline. They will also ask how you will be using the money, though in a real estate loan, it will be obvious for the most part. If you are hoping to have additional money for renovations or improvements, these may be covered with either a separate loan or side-riders, giving you a possible advantage if you are able to pay them off early.

You'll want to think about how you want to set up your business. After all, purchasing CRE property is a business, and taking any shortcuts here will surely put you in a disastrous place. So, let's discuss a few things you may want to consider when setting up your business and applying for a loan.

Before searching for a good lender for your investment, you should also know these numbers and calculations, if you want to stay on top of the game and analyze your CRE investment properties effectively. We've discussed these briefly, but here is the bottom line about what you need to know and why you need to know it.

INDIVIDUAL OR ENTITY?

Are you thinking you'll be investing alone, or will you have a partner? Or, perhaps, will several of you contribute to the investment?

You may feel like a purchase of a CRE property would naturally be by a corporation, developer, or partnership, but quite often, individuals are the leading demographic when obtaining initial CRE loans. You may be asked to provide a bit more personal history than an established business, but in the long run, getting a loan, either as an individual or an entity, can be a similar process.

If this is your first investment loan, or if your partnership or business is fairly new, an investigator will be appointed to verify and conduct any additional verification which may be required. The guarantee of the loan is, after all, up to the lender. It is the lender's responsibility to ask the needed questions and get the supporting information to complete the process. It will be up to you (and your associates if applicable) to supply the required documentation and make sure everything is current, stated correctly, and organized for the lender's representative in the best possible manner.

LOAN TO VALUE RATIO (LTV)

As we've discussed earlier, the loan to value ratio is a basic metric many, if not all, lenders use in determining your ability to repay the loan. Even though the lender would assume the property if you default, lenders aren't in the real estate business, nor do they want to be. They would much rather have your money than your property, so they will make sure you are a good risk for them to take before offering you a loan.

Because the LTV measures the value of the loan

compared to the value of the property, it is a highly-regarded calculation used for your loan decision. You'll want to make sure you can cover the down payment easily if required, and have all documentation accessible and easy to understand. Commercial loans generally range from 65% to 80%, depending on where the property is located and what other criteria plays into the property's value.

Just an FYI, lower LTV properties often qualify for more favorable rates for financing than properties with a higher LTV.

DEBT-SERVICE COVERAGE RATIO

Because this figure directly evaluates the ability of your property's income to pay back your loan, the DSCR plays an integral part in determining your loan decision.

You will want to determine this factor before going into a lender, and quite frankly, it should be one of the first calculations you do on a property to see if it is a good value and investment to begin with.

$$DSCR = NOI / debt\ service$$

ADDITIONAL INCOME

Another way you can produce extra income is to raise the money for your property yourself. By doing so, you may be entitled to charge an acquisition fee during the closing of the investment purchase.

Typically, acquisition fees are 3% of the purchase price, and can help offset other expenses you may be looking at for renovations, updates, marketing for tenants, or a long vacation you feel you may be entitled to after all is said and done!

Be sure to discuss this with your team of professionals to make sure all the details are in place.

CHAPTER SUMMARY

- CRE property lending is different, offering many benefits and advantages, depending on the intent of the prospective owner of the property, their investment goals, and the history of the investor.
- The probability of securing a loan is based on many factors, and if these factors are assessed favorably, the applicant has a good chance for loan acceptance and lower interest rates.

In the next chapter, you will learn the intricacies of management companies and what you need to know when deciding to either hire one or assume the role yourself.

CHAPTER SIX: STEP THREE - MANAGING AND MAINTAINING YOUR INVESTMENTS

❉❉❉

Now, let's imagine you've purchased your first investment property.

How can you be an effective property owner and still be able to maintain a happy and productive life for yourself?

Often, CRE owners and investors tend to get a bit of anxiety when they purchase their first property. Though they want a 'hands-on' experience by seeing how their investment is growing, they find themselves overworked and overwhelmed.

Knowledge you will want to gain so you can decide whether to oversee the management of your property yourself or whether you should hire an agency to manage it should include:

- Active rental of property and units.
- Terms needed within a lease agreement and the procurement thereof.
- Tenant occupancy and lease management.
- Property risk.
- Maintenance (both of the property and buildings).

If you feel you can manage any or all of these jobs, great. You may have had prior experience in one or all of these fields and are looking to your property as your 'job'. But if you haven't, realize the management of commercial properties can be a polar opposite to managing residential real estate.

Do a bit of investigation and connect with an experienced property manager. This relationship will be an 'initiation' of sorts and can teach you all the ins and outs of keeping your property well maintained and in turn, keep your tenants happy. You'll also want to invest in a good software program to study net leasing, common area maintenance (CAM), costs, and contracts. You'll also want to speak with your team real estate agent for lease and agreement term statements. By delegating your management, you will gain valuable time and reduce your mistakes which, without gaining the education, can cost you valuable profits and expected revenue.

If you are feeling the burden of management is too great and you are seeing the stress of it seeping into areas of your personal life, a management agency may be the answer to your salvation.

By hiring someone else to govern and manage your investment, you can take a step back and enjoy the life you had imagined prior to your investment purchase. No longer do you have to answer the phone for an electrical failure or a loud tenant. Your management team will take care of the problem, and so much more.

The agency can be as involved as you wish. The factors determining this involvement can be as broad as your imagination, or determined by the time you want to spend managing your property. Many investors put the deal together and hire out an agency to manage the rest, so they can move forward with putting another investment together to replicate the first.

When you hire an agency for management, you aren't just looking to ease your own life, but also to increase the well-being of your tenants. There are several ways you can achieve this balance, and it doesn't have to involve other people.

Some believe having technology can take care of their management needs, for example in a warehouse or storage facility. This can not only be an advantageous feature when looking for renters but it will set a tenant's mind at ease after signing the lease to know there are features such as electronic security.

If buildings need to be monitored, as with office buildings and apartment complexes a management company can help with this. You want to focus on a person or company with specific skills which can be used to oversee your property in ways you can't do yourself.

If you choose to hire an agency to manage your properties, make sure you get these items in place. Basic skills your management agency should possess include:

- Time management.
- Computer skills.
- Legal documentation.
- Negotiation skills.
- Marketing.
- Financial controls.
- Client relations.
- Property knowledge.

IF YOU ARE LOOKING FOR A HANDS-ON EXPERIENCE

If you have a business occupying your properties, you'll want to *collect sales and tax returns* of those tenants. If you see the rent is higher than 6% to 8% of their revenue, you may want to investigate further into their financial stability. Make sure their assets can cover any guarantees or lease agreements if the company has to declare bankruptcy.

When negotiating a tenancy, always get a *personal guarantee* in place. Be thorough with this, as you want your tenant to treat your property as well as you would. It is similar to having a security deposit and a personal contract. If they don't have a company or any added associates behind their tenancy, make sure you receive a *business balance sheet* to support their personal guarantee. If you see they don't have the funding or assets to back up their lease, a tenant default with no recourse may be your end result.

If you are considering hiring an agency to acquire tenants, you've probably already realized you can't do this all yourself. Along with this realization, you need to understand that your management agency, if you've done your due diligence, are the *experts at maintaining your property and its wellbeing*. Let them do their job. If you've done your homework and have concluded that they are a reputable agency, rest assured, your property is being managed well. All you have to do at this point is to keep an eye on the upkeep.

Some investors have narrowed their property investments to only purchasing on a triple net lease (NNN) which has strong national or regional tenants. This may be your business strategy also. With this type of purchase, you are not responsible for such things as insurance, taxes, and upkeep. Refer back to the earlier sections which detail this, but if you were leaning towards this type of property investment, you may also save yourself anxiety when contemplating management of the property, since it will be the responsibility of your tenant.

When you hire an agency, you may feel you might become detached from your investment and want to be more involved in its growth and tenant management. Not only is this a fairly common occurrence, but your feelings are definitely justified.

By *developing a relationship with your tenants* you are keeping a door open for communication, and you won't feel like your tenants are expendable. In other words, you will go out of your way to keep them happy and they, in turn, will be more content and feel obliged to keep your property well-maintained. As I said earlier, developing these relationships can open unseen doors for you, creating additional avenues of wealth.

Invest in technology on your property. This will more than pay for itself in the long run. By having a monitoring system or systems in place, you will be able to see immediately what your utility use is, what average costs are for the laundry facility, or compare the use and costs of tenants using amenities from season to season.

Though your agency may be a national company, make sure the *manager who actually does the work resides in the area*, hopefully within 20 minutes of your property. By having this person within a close driving distance, they will not only be able to address tenant needs quickly, but they can easily monitor your property on a regular basis.

When comparing agencies and managers, be sure to *ask for licenses and certifications* which may relate to their business. Each one differs, but the management agency will know what you are asking for and what you need for your specific property. If they don't, move on to another service provider.

Also, check out other properties they manage to see how they look, how they're run, and talk to tenants to see if they are happy with their facilities and its upkeep.

Remember to *keep records produced by your property manager for profit and loss* (P&L) entries on your financials and tax records. Your accountant will be looking for these too, but it's a good idea to keep updated on them for your own benefit, making sure all expenses are justified.

STAY UPDATED ON YOUR PROPERTY

As you monitor your property's growth, make sure you are updating the rent on each unit as it becomes available or when the lease is due for renewal. You'll want to do a quick comparison with like properties and see what the going rates are and adjust yours accordingly. Keep within the attractive brackets to make sure you are making the highest rate possible while still attracting viable tenants.

YOUR TENANTS' BUSINESSES WILL GROW TOO

As your tenants thrive and grow, they may need to move to a larger space. Consider moving these kinds of tenants into larger units. If they are happy with you as a landlord but are thinking they've grown out of their space, offer them a good deal on another unit which will accommodate their growth. If it isn't available readily, notify them of the next available unit and try to negotiate a working move-in date. By taking the time to keep a good tenant, you will not only keep them happy and feeling appreciated, but you will be maintaining your existing, great business relationship and save paperwork and risk down the road.

IS YOUR COMPETITION OFFERING MORE?

Check your competition to see what differs between your rental property and theirs. Have they made improvements which seem to be taking your business away? Stay on top of the trends in your neighborhood and make prudent and necessary upgrades to stay competitive and efficient.

DECREASE INITIAL EXPENSES

When you began this venture, you realized there was a lot to learn. Just as with purchasing and investing in real estate, there is a learning curve with managing a property.

As you improve in your abilities, keep a close eye on the operating expenses of your property. Chances are, as you get to know your investment, you will be able to see where your dollars are best spent and also, if possible, where you can cut some costs. It all comes down to the bottom line for investments, and the more they return revenue back to you, the sooner you will be looking at your freedom from financial obligations.

EXPLORE POSSIBLE INCOME-PRODUCING IDEAS

Will installing a laundry facility improve your property's value? Maybe having a nice landscaped outside luncheon area for employees to relax enables you to increase your rental rates? Stay on the cutting edge by improving your property with either needed amenities or by satisfying additional tenant desires. Give your competition something to envy. By reinvesting in your own property in useful and profitable ways, you will be leading the community for property appeal and attractiveness.

PROPERTY AND INCOME TAXES

I hate to say it, but *property taxes* are an inevitable part of investment. While none of us are keen on the topic, using all the tools you can to keep them as low as possible gives you an edge and can contribute to the value of each investment.

Though we've already discussed the importance of having a CPA and tax advisor on your team, it would be to your benefit to know how they affect you and your investments with regard to future planning and strategies. Each location will be different in its tax structure and will include taxes due to various levels of government.

- Property taxes.
- Federal income taxes on net income of your investments.
- State income taxes on net income of your properties.
- Local taxes on net income of investments.

TAX BENEFITS

Yes, there is a silver lining to the storm clouds of taxes, and it can be significant. You've learned these benefits are actually what make CRE investing such a wonderful option for portfolio growth. Consider these advantages up close:

- The interest on commercial mortgages is tax-deductible.
- The IRS allows CRE investors to claim depreciation as a tax deduction.
- Non-mortgage expenses can be tax-deductible, including repairs, management expenses, renovations, and CAM fees. There are more, which you can discover when you research your specific property locations.
- The tax rate on capital gains is most often at a lower rate than personal income tax, giving you extensive savings when you sell a property.
- The capital gains you receive from one property sale can also quickly be invested into another property by using a *1035 exchange form* on your

income tax report. Your advisor can determine the turn-around time needed.
- The benefactors of your CRE investments, if they decide to sell, will only pay tax on the increased value of the property at the time of inheritance.
- Qualified business income can be a tax deduction. Again, follow the advice of your CPA and tax advisor.
- You receive federal tax credits on certain types of CRE properties.
- CRE losses can be claimed as deductions.

IF YOUR BUSINESS IS AN LLC

Since 2018, a 20% deduction on income is allowed if it is received as a pass-through entity, such as with your LLC business profile.

I've said this before and I cannot stress it enough, contact a reliable tax advisor and CPA to help you maximize these benefits and find more ways to reduce your business costs.

INSURANCE

Though an LLC protects your personal assets from liability claims and it is more advantageous than liability insurance, there are other items which need insurance coverage if you are to have a sound CRE investment which keeps on bringing in revenue and good tenants.

This money is well spent, whether you have claims for the insurance or not. Once again, do the research on your location and make sure you aren't over-protecting your property from risks which are unnecessary.

Liability Insurance: Accidents do happen, and being in the position of needing coverage without having it can be a liability to you and your portfolio. If you have a tenant whose customers are at risk, perhaps a medical clinic or convalescent home, you may want to have an extra carrier in place. There are many instances where having this coverage would be to your advantage. Talk with your CRE team and compare the advantages to the cost to determine if it fits your needs. If you've set up your business as an LLC, your needs could be adequately covered, but you should analyze your risks fully and then make the decision.

Loss of Income for Landlords During Times of Rental Vacancies: This is an additional rider which can come in handy if you find you have a tenant who has abused your property (damage repairs can take time), or have a sudden default on a lease. If you have diligently put funds away in a contingency fund, then you may be covered. If, however, you feel extra money may be needed for periodic repair of expensive investment properties or multiple levels of sub-leases, take a second look at this insurance.

Flood Insurance: Just as it is stated, it can cover damage done after a flood. If the property is deemed to lie in a 'flood zone', it may be advisable to get flood insurance. This insurance can also be a requirement of your business loan, and if it is not acquired or in place when a flood occurs, it can send your loan into default, requiring balances to be paid immediately. Your financial institution will be aware of whether it is needed for your transaction. This insurance also covers broken pipes, which is an item that is often overlooked.

Builder's Risk Insurance: This insurance covers property which is being renovated or is under construction, and it covers the workers as well as any vandalism which may occur during the construction of the property. It is expensive insurance, up to four times as expensive as normal hazard or fire insurance, but it can be a lifesaver if the building burns down in a fire or foundations sink due to contractor oversights.

General Contractor's Insurance: If you're interested in applying for your own permits on a renovation or construction project, you will need to get a contractor's license, as well as this insurance, which covers any discrepancies which may occur during the construction process. Check-in with local agencies to determine what you need.

Worker's Compensation: This is a federal fund which needs to be paid by all employers who pay salaries to their workers, unless they are contractors or consultants. If a person is injured while 'on the job', then the medical costs of the injury will be paid by the fund the employer has been paying into.

KEEP YOUR PORTFOLIO UPDATED

It's true, we all get distracted with our lives and the distractions of the day-to-day, but just because you have purchased your property and things are humming along nicely, doesn't mean it can't be whirring along at a much more profitable pace.

Keep updated on your property investments as well as their neighborhoods and values. Construct exit strategies on all your investments, in case you find you need to liquidate quickly or suddenly have a large sum you need to invest to defer taxes.

Exit strategies can include a standard sale of property through a CRE agent, selling the property 'by owner', providing seller financing to the buyer at a rate which doesn't extend your necessity to sell, lease option utilization (restating agreements), or using a 1031 exchange form on your tax returns. A few other proven ways to get out from under a purchase could involve a sale or lease buyback, gifting your property to a benefactor or heir, refinancing the property (possible equity or financial funding advantage), wholesale the property for purchase, or 'flip' the contract for a quick sale.

Going through the numbers and determining viable means for liquidation at various points in time can also give you a clear picture of how your property is appreciating, and if it is delivering at the projected level you were expecting when you originally purchased it.

By *comparing your investment goals* to your property performance often, you guard yourself against new risks and unseen fluctuations in the economy. After all, the performance of your investment is the path to achieving your financial freedom - watch it closely and adjust it as needed.

WATCH YOUR PORTFOLIO GROW

Finally, you can begin to watch your revenue build, your accounts gain in value, and your portfolio increase in size and profitability. It's been a process, hasn't it? What rewards await you at the end of each investment? Not only money, which is why you originally began this quest, but also the satisfaction of being in control of your money, your future, and your freedom.

Your investment path is now clear and you have seen how all the small details fall into place and give you a larger picture of how to achieve success. Always play by the rules outlined below, and you will be victorious in any investment you care to make!

- Start with one good investment. Run the figures, do the analysis, and determine your price for the property.
- Always buy below market value. This gives you an equity advantage the moment you accept the keys.

- Make money when you buy. Use all the tools which are available to you, from acquisition fees to cash-on-cash returns.
- Shop with your imagination. Don't limit yourself to traditional or common property types. Keep the special types of CRE properties in the mix to broaden your scope and find the best deals.
- Buy at the right time. Sometimes the market is up, and sometimes the location has pending zoning changes. Make sure you know about changes that may affect the value of a CRE in the future.
- Avoid cross-collateralization. Don't use cash advantages with several tools. Keep your finances simple and always make sure your financial advisor is at hand and approves.
- Work closely with your team. Legal counsel, CPA, real estate agent, broker, and a tax advisor are all people who can help guide you to prosperity and success with your CRE investment.
- Research, research, research! Property, location, history of occupancy, and proposed public projects nearby should all be topics that you know inside and out.
- Delight your tenants. By keeping a cordial and open communication style with your tenants, you are not only making sure they are happy and well taken care of, but you are extending your business network to develop opportunities and new avenues of income.
- Remember the 1% rule. The 1% rule determines if the rental revenue from a property will exceed the mortgage payment, with 1% above the break-even mark being the lowest you will accept.

CHAPTER SUMMARY

- Just because you have completed the property purchase doesn't mean you have finished the deal. Management of your properties is essential to keep them in peak shape. This will result in the highest possible revenue throughout your ownership.
- Continually use the basics you've learned to stay updated on techniques for CRE analysis and purchase.

CONCLUSIONS AND GLOSSARY

WELL, HERE YOU ARE! YOU'VE COMPLETED THE BOOK AND CAN now, confidently, move forward and achieve your CRE lifestyle and financial freedom.

As you already know, the more you use the concepts and strategies in this book, the more natural all of these ideologies will become. You'll be able to determine a CAP or DSR from just looking at the figures. This will all happen sooner than you can imagine!

Please click Michael Steven Facebook Page for more information and further reading material from me.

If you have any questions and would like to connect, or you want to keep up on my latest and greatest, please email me at Connect with Michael Steven. I'd love to hear about your experiences and successes!

For your quick reference, I've also listed some useful terms and definitions below. Some we've talked about, others you may come across in your own research.

Assignment clause (or novation clause): This clause determines whether rights, obligations and/or duties, under an agreement, can be transferred, in whole or in part, to another party. This clause can also list specific conditions or limitations.

Building Classifications: A rating of building conditions for comparison purposes between properties. Classes are as follows:

- *Class A*: These are the newest and highest quality properties, with the best locations and the highest rents.
- *Class B*: An older structure than Class A, but it still has good qualities which attract average, working-class tenants. Class B buildings in a good location can be returned to their Class A glory with minimal renovations.
- *Class C*: This is the lowest official classification. These buildings are older and need updating. They have the lowest rents and cater to lower to middle-income tenants. If you are an apartment investor, Class C is the way to go because the ratio between the price per unit and the rental income is still good, providing the highest returns. However, these buildings will need a lot of maintenance, and the neighborhoods and tenants can be challenging.
- *Class D*: Although this is not an official class, this term is often used to refer to vacant buildings in need of extensive renovation.

Common area maintenance (CAM) fees: These are costs billed to tenants in a triple net (NNN) lease, and they are paid by tenants to the landlord of a CRE. This is in addition to rent. It can be used to pay for anything from carpets, pool maintenance or hallway painting to parking area resurfacing.

Escalator clause: This clause allows for an increase or decrease in wages or prices under certain conditions. It can allow you to state that you have made an offer, but if you are outbid or undercut, you have the option to increase or decrease your offer.

Landlord representative: This leasing agent represents the best interests of the landlord or building owner when marketing and leasing rentals on behalf of the landlord.

Letter of intent (LOI): A document which states a preliminary commitment of one party to do business with another, outlining any details or necessities.

Option to buy: This is an arrangement or agreement made between the landlord and the tenant or investor, to acquire a rented property with an option to purchase in the future. Terms and conditions are outlined within the agreement.

Parking ratio: This ratio is used mostly in office building descriptions, and it is calculated by dividing the total rentable square footage of a property by the number of parking spaces available. It's most often expressed in square feet. Example: A building with 40,000 square feet and 180 parking spaces has a parking ratio of 4.5 spaces per 1,000 square feet.

Referral fee: A fee which is paid when one agent or broker refers a client to another agent or broker based on the eventual commission when the sale closes. Most range between 20% to 35%.

Rent concessions: Enticements made to a rental applicant to entice them to rent, such as a free month of occupancy or a reduced security deposit.

Rentable square footage: This square footage includes outside areas around tenant units, such as pool and community areas, and is added to the square footage the tenant occupies.

Right of expansion: This clause gives a renter an option to add additional space to a rented property. It should be specific about what will be accepted in the expansion.

Right of first refusal (ROFR or RFR): This contractual right gives its holder the option to do business with an owner of collateral before another party can enter into the transaction. Think of it as a 'first right to purchase' offer.

Sublease clause (or contract): Allows the original tenant of a rental property the option to rent all or partial areas of a property to another tenant, known as a subtenant.

Tenant improvements: Any change made by a tenant on a rented property is considered a tenant improvement, and it usually requires a permit. It can range from altering a property to meet the tenant's needs to upgrading plumbing or mechanical systems.

Tenant representative: A representative who facilitates the lease agreement between a tenant and the landlord, and is often referred to as a broker.

Usable square footage: Used in every property description, this is the total amount of area in a building or unit that a tenant occupies, and it is used as a contributing factor in other calculations and comparisons.

Vacancy rate: This is the number of available units within a building that are available for rent (apartments, hotels, etc.).

∽

IF YOU ENJOYED READING MY BOOK, PLEASE LEAVE ME A POSITIVE REVIEW, THIS WOULD BE GREATLY APPRECIATED. Email me a copy of your Review and it might be selected to appear in the "EDITORIAL SECTION" on Amazon. **EMAIL: michael@TheBestSellerBooks.com**

FINAL WORDS

❊❊❊

If you'd like to dig deeper into CRE investing and gain a few different angles on the process, I'd suggest the articles listed below, and encourage you to visit my website at Michael Steven.

Further Reading

What Coronavirus Slowdown?
https://www.bisnow.com/dallas-ft-worth/news/commercial-real-estate/what-covid-19-slowdown-allen-commercial-development-soars-during-pandemic-105749

Break Down Your Mortgage Payment
https://www.fortunebuilders.com/breaking-down-the-5-aspects-of-a-mortgage-payment/

8 Numbers to Know for Your Property Value Estimator
https://www.fortunebuilders.com/property-value-estimator/

ARV Meaning & Calculator for Investors
https://www.fortunebuilders.com/what-is-arv-meaning-how-to-calculate-your-investment/

Tips for Calculating Square Footage in a Home
https://www.fortunebuilders.com/calculating-square-footage/

CHECK OUT MY OTHER BOOKS!

FINANCIAL FREEDOM with REAL ESTATE

START MAKING MONEY TODAY BECAUSE EVERYONE ELSE IS

3 SIMPLE WAYS THAT EVEN YOUR KIDS CAN DO IT:
SECRETS GUARANTEED TO WORK RIGHT AWAY

MICHAEL STEVEN

https://www.amazon.com/dp/B08DVD8XWX

https://www.amazon.com/dp/B08KHK5N2

Visit my Amazon Author Page

https://www.amazon.com/~/e/B08F814H2

REAL ESTATE INVESTMENT CHECKLIST

(9 Calculators That Will Help You Achieve Success!)

This checklist includes:

❑ 9 important calculators that you should use to achieve success and head towards *Financial Freedom with Real Estate*

❑ Helpful links

❑ Plus receive future updates

Forget about yesterday and start thinking about tomorrow.

"The past and the future are separated by a second, so make that second count!" ~ Quote from Carmine Pirone

To receive your Free Real Estate Calculators Checklist, email me at:

michael@TheBestSellerBooks.com

REFERENCES

[1]Merrill, T. *10 Real estate calculators every investor should know*. Fortune Builders. found on 09.22.2020 at https://www.fortunebuilders.com/real-estate-calculator/

[2] Investopedia.com . definition 'GDP' - https://www.investopedia.com/terms/g/gdp.asp

Bisnow

https://www.bisnow.com

https://www.bisnow.com/dallas-ft-worth/news/commercial-real-estate/the-trajectory-of-construction-costs-varies-depending-on-where-you-are-and-what-youre-building-105759

CBRE

https://www.cbre.com/research-results?k= fesibility%20study

Coach Carson

https://www.coachcarson.com

Commercial Loan Direct

https://www.commercialloandirect.com/debt-service-coverage-ratio-calculator.html

Commercial Real Estate Online
https://commercial-realestate-training.com/the-6-basic-principles-of-commercial-prop
erty-management/
Contract Standards
https://www.contractstandards.com/public/clauses/assignment

Deloitte Insights
https://www2.deloitte.com/us/en/pages/real-estate/articles/commercial-real-estate-industry-outlook.html
Forbes
https://www.forbes.com/sites/jordanlulich/2018/07/29/important-commercial-real-estate-terms-you-should-known/#3bf8be119e6f
Fortune Builders
https://www.fortunebuilders.com/how-to-invest-in-commercial-real-estate-getting-started/
https://www.fortunebuilders.com/real-estate-calculator/
https://www.forbes.com/sites/jordanlulich/2018/07/29/important-commercial-real-estate-terms-you-should-known/#3bf8be119e6f
Investopedia
https://www.investopedia.com/terms/o/one-percent-rule.asp
Legalzoom - Jeff Walker, Esq.
https://www.legalzoom.com/articles/forming-an-llc-for-real-estate-investments-pros-cons
Live Oak Bank
https://www.liveoakbank.com/live-oak-bank-resources/5-cs-of-credit-analysis-3/

Mash Advisor
https://www.mashvisor.com/blog/pro-forma-real-estate-guide/

MillionAcres - A Motley Fool Service
https://www.fool.com/millionacres/real-estate-investing/commercial-real-estate/6-things-you-need-know-investing-commercial-real-estate/

Prospectus - Strategic Capital Growth
https://www.prospectus.com/feasibility-study-for-real-estate/

Ramey King Insurance
https://rameyking.com/6-types-insurance-commercial-real-estate-investor/

Realized 1031
http://www.realized1031.com/glossary/parking-ratio

US News
https://www.usnews.com/news/cities/slideshows/the-10-best-cities-for-jobs

Westwood Net Lease
https://westwoodnetlease.com/14-commercial-real-estate-terms/

Yield Finda
https://www.yieldfinda.com/commercial-real-estate/factors-consider-buying-commercial-property/

IF YOU ENJOYED READING MY BOOK, PLEASE LEAVE ME A POSITIVE REVIEW, THIS WOULD BE GREATLY APPRECIATED. Email me a copy of your Review and it might be selected to appear in the "EDITORIAL SECTION" on Amazon.
EMAIL: michael@TheBestSellerBooks.com

Printed in Great Britain
by Amazon